ARE YOU READY TO CHANGE?

Living an Abundant Christian Life

MICHAEL E. FRISINA

WESTBOW
PRESS®
A DIVISION OF THOMAS NELSON
& ZONDERVAN

Copyright © 2016 Michael E. Frisina

All rights reserved. No part of this book may be used or reproduced by any means, graphic, electronic, or mechanical, including photocopying, recording, taping or by any information storage retrieval system without the written permission of the author except in the case of brief quotations embodied in critical articles and reviews.

Scripture taken from the New King James Version. Copyright © 1979, 1980, 1982 by Thomas Nelson, Inc. Used by permission. All rights reserved.

This book is a work of non-fiction. Unless otherwise noted, the author and the publisher make no explicit guarantees as to the accuracy of the information contained in this book and in some cases, names of people and places have been altered to protect their privacy.

Disclaimer: The information and solutions offered in this book are intended to serve as guidelines and application of Bible principles. None of what is written in this book is meant to substitute for specific medical interventions from licensed care providers. Readers should discuss specific behavior symptoms and medical conditions with their licensed care providers and practitioners.

Every effort has been made to use cited material from the identified resource list as required for copyrighted material. The author and publisher apologize for any errors or omissions and would be grateful if notified of any corrections that should be incorporated in future reprints or editions of this book.

WestBow Press books may be ordered through booksellers or by contacting:

WestBow Press
A Division of Thomas Nelson & Zondervan
1663 Liberty Drive
Bloomington, IN 47403
www.westbowpress.com
1 (866) 928-1240

Because of the dynamic nature of the Internet, any web addresses or links contained in this book may have changed since publication and may no longer be valid. The views expressed in this work are solely those of the author and do not necessarily reflect the views of the publisher, and the publisher hereby disclaims any responsibility for them.

Any people depicted in stock imagery provided by Thinkstock are models, and such images are being used for illustrative purposes only. Certain stock imagery © Thinkstock.

ISBN: 978-1-5127-2854-5 (sc)
ISBN: 978-1-5127-2855-2 (hc)
ISBN: 978-1-5127-2853-8 (e)

Library of Congress Control Number: 2016901348

Print information available on the last page.

WestBow Press rev. date: 03/30/2016

Contents

Acknowledgments ix
Introduction xi

PART I   **The Most Important Thing You Need to Believe** 1
     1   Are You Ready to Change? 7
     2   Why You Struggle to Change 18
     3   How You Can Change 37

PART II   **Knowing Yourself and Managing Yourself Well** 47
     4   Change Your Heart and Change Your Mind 53
     5   Change Your Mind and Change Your Beliefs 63
     6   Change Your Beliefs and Change Your Behavior 81

PART III   **Knowing Yourself and Managing Yourself Well with Others** 99
     7   Manage Your Emotions 103
     8   Manage Your Communication 122
     9   Manage Your Relationships 136
    10   Read This Last 151

Appendix 1: Social / Behavioral Styles under Stress 153
Appendix 2: Assess the Trust Levels in Your Team Relationships .. 156
References 159
About the Author 161

This book is dedicated to the congregation of Calvary Chapel Northeast Columbia. You have given me the privilege and the honor of being your spiritual leader. It is a responsibility that I do not take lightly. My prayer and hope each day is that you read and study the Word of God and that you commit to living it every day of your life in your own behavior.

You are a wonderful group of people, and I am thankful that I get to live out my life's purpose with you every day, using my enthusiasm and optimism to inspire and motivate you to become the best you can be in conforming to the image of Jesus Christ. Together we can go and change the world for good.

Acknowledgments

You will hear people say that the hardest book to write is the first one. While the process of writing may become less work, the process of finishing a book remains the tireless effort of a host of people. That said, I take full responsibility for anything that may be wrong with this book, and I give credit to all the following people for what makes it worth reading.

First, I must acknowledge my wife, Susan. She has endured my behavior lapses and growth for over thirty-six years. Her love for God and devotion to living an abundant life in Christ has inspired me every day from the first moment we met.

My children, Michael, Robert, and Rebekah, are a living testament to the principles of this book. Despite my many mistakes as your father, each of you has persevered through your own personal struggles and growth to become wonderful parents, successful adults, and committed believers to the gospel of Jesus Christ. No father could be more proud.

As I said in the dedication, I acknowledge the people who comprise the congregation of Calvary Chapel Northeast Columbia. You never cease to amaze me with your talents, your commitment, your perseverance, and your courage to face challenging life events with unwavering faith in the love and devotion of our heavenly Father. Thank you once again for how you honor me.

To my editing assistants, Renee Lucido and Rosanne Mir, thank you for your time and talents to read and edit the drafts of this book. Without your effort, the quality of this book would have been lost. Thank you for your hard work and for your friendship.

Finally, thank you to the professional staff of WestBow Press. Your contribution to this project was essential in bringing this book to life. Jenn Seiler, many thanks for your patience and for not giving up on me when it seemed like I would not finish writing. Maurice Broaddus, thank you for your continued effort to contact me and encourage me to finish this book. Without your consistent encouragement, I may never have found the motivation to complete it.

Introduction

Organization of the Book

You are not reading a self-help book. This book teaches you how to apply biblical principles to your life choices to attain self-mastery. The apostle Paul wrote, "Do not be conformed to this world, but be transformed by the renewing of your mind, that you may prove what is that good and acceptable and perfect will of God" (Rom. 12:2). We all understand that we are to be transformed by getting a new mind, but how does that work in practical terms?

This book will teach you what to do, practically speaking. It will teach you how to become self-aware, how to construct biblical mental models that guide how you think, how you behave, and ultimately how you influence the consequences and events that frame your life. In that sense, as a book of self-mastery, it is organized around several key, foundational truths from the Holy Bible. Our heavenly Father has already provided for us all the knowledge and gifts we need to live a victorious life in Jesus Christ. Just as He provided all the artisans with the knowledge, skills, talents, and resources to build the tabernacle in the wilderness, so too, our heavenly Father has provided for us to build our own spiritual tabernacles to be inhabited by Him. In that sense, this book is all about your personal transformational journey into the character, image, and likeness of Jesus Christ.

To guide you on this journey, this book will provide you with six biblical principles (contained in parts II and III) that frame the foundation for creating and sustaining an abundant life in Jesus Christ. You will learn how to:

- Put your heart and mind into a physical connection to great inner peace and more productive and creative thinking
- Use your power to control your thoughts to manage your behavior choices
- Change your beliefs and behavior to change your circumstances and outcomes
- Manage emotions effectively to obey the command to "be anxious for nothing"
- Improve your ability to communicate more effectively with others and to create productive, emotional connections with others
- Develop and sustain highly effective relationships that will be critical to your living a life more abundantly in Jesus Christ.

As many other writers have discovered over the years—including King Solomon and the apostle Paul—what you choose to think about and believe determines not only the quality of life you achieve but ultimately the characteristics that define who you become as a person. King Solomon encourages us to guard our hearts, for from them flows what guides our life. The apostle Paul wrote, "Whatever things are true, whatever things are noble, whatever things are just, whatever things are pure, whatever things are lovely, whatever things are of good report, if there is any virtue and if there is anything praiseworthy—meditate on these things" (Phil. 4:8).

What you will learn in this book has worked for countless individuals who have been diligent to learn and apply these principles to their daily lives. They will work for you too. Here again is the "power principle" from which the abundant life is derived. If you will change what you believe, you will change your life. An abiding life in Jesus Christ is meant to be fruitful and abundant. While our salvation in Christ is complete in the cross, the way we choose to live after that salvation experience requires our active participation.

This book is all about teaching you how to engage with the key principles that create a fulfilled life in Jesus Christ. Allowing the fruit of the Spirit to manifest itself in your life requires you to replace old, disruptive, toxic, destructive thinking patterns with new, positive, supportive, productive ones. Part I, and the next chapter specifically, will explain why we resist change and fail to change, even though change is possible for everyone. The third chapter will give you new knowledge that will help to persuade you that change is possible for you.

Part II of the book gives you three guiding principles for guarding your heart. Part III provides you with three guiding principles to guard your mind. Together these two sets of life principles provide you with tangible guidance for daily living. When I am aware and stay connected to my inner core values, I have the means to choose wisely between productive thoughts and unproductive thoughts. I have the means to choose between biblical thoughts and worldly thoughts. When I focus on my compelling purpose statement, which gets me out of bed in the morning with great passion, I am better able to resist the temptation to take shortcuts and to accept short-term rewards that often come with long-term consequences.

In 2 Peter 1:3–11, we are instructed to create spiritual discipline in our lives. You have a personal responsibility and are accountable to God the Father, Himself, for your spiritual maturation. You must partner with the Holy Spirit to bring change into your life that is God-breathed and God-ordained for you. The idea that you are living life with consequences of your own making may be both puzzling and disturbing to you at the moment. This is a natural response if you have never been exposed to the concept that "as a man thinks, so he is." Keep in mind that change, even change we desire, always meets with mental, emotional, and physical resistance.

As you ponder making significant changes in your life, it is natural to feel a sense of fear, loss, and doubt. You will learn how to overcome this natural response with purposeful and intentional choices that propel you to new learning, discovery, and integration of these principles, and you will immediately begin to benefit from them. You will learn that you can have abundant life with Jesus Christ. Are you ready to change?

PART I

The Most Important Thing You Need to Believe

And do not be conformed to this world, but be transformed by the renewing of your mind, so that you may prove what the will of God is, that which is good and acceptable and perfect.
—Romans 12:2

The hardest thing is not to get people to accept new ideas but to get them to forget old ones.
—John Maynard Keys

What would you like to change about you? Have you ever tried to change an ineffective habit? Has your boss or your spouse ever told you that something about you has to change? Have you ever had a moment when you told yourself that something about you needs to change? If you answered yes to at least one of these questions, then you are reading a book that was written just for you. Now, the most important thing you need to believe is that you *can* change!

No matter where you are in your journey through life, you will encounter something about yourself—a thought, a belief, or a behavior—that needs to change. I'm referring to changing a habit that is holding you back in your spiritual life. Or perhaps it is a habit change that is required to live a healthier physical life. We all have opportunities to change in areas of our professional lives in order to lead more effectively, be more supportive team members, and make work and life more meaningful and fulfilling.

The primary objective of this book is to provide you with practical tools that will enable you to part ways with old, ineffective, and often destructive thoughts, emotions, ineffective habits, and self-limiting behaviors. Your willingness to break with your current habits will allow you to acquire new habits where you can experience higher levels of achievement, performance outcomes, and peace of mind in your walk with Jesus Christ. You will learn tangible, reasonable, and practical tools you can apply to your thoughts, emotions, attitudes, and behavior to improve your effectiveness in all three levels of relationships: to your heavenly Father, others, and yourself.

New research continues to emerge, reinforcing the truth of older research: that successful change requires focused mental, emotional, physical, and spiritual commitment. Successful change requires a clear sense of purpose and passionate desire. Successful change also requires a great deal of dissatisfaction with the status quo: living with your current thoughts, beliefs, and behaviors and the outcomes and consequences they are producing for you. Successful change also requires being able to do something new that is practical, doable, and achievable.

We all have made resolutions and promises to change ineffective thoughts, beliefs, and behaviors. Everyone tends to start with good intentions, but those who actually achieve significant and sustained change are in the minority. Simply look at the fitness center parking lot in January, and then compare it to what you see at the end of February.

Here is good news for you. Successful changers do not have any special magic creating effective and sustained change in their lives. What they have is the knowledge and a system for change that, when applied consistently, passionately, and without compromise, produces the change they were seeking in their lives. The good news is that you can be one of these people too!

This book is a result of my own unpredictable journey through life. By constantly submitting my will and life choices to the plan and purpose my heavenly Father had in mind for me, I am fulfilling His plan for my life every day. By submitting your will to the will of the Father, you will discover and fulfill the plan and purpose He has for your life as well. The key to life is not how many times we get knocked down but how many times we get back up. There is a little Korean lady named Cha-Sa-Soon. I have read that her name literally means "get knocked down six times, get up seven." To enhance her little business, Cha-Sa-Soon decided she wanted to get a driver's license. She failed the test over and over again, but she refused to quit. Finally, after 760 attempts, she passed. Is there anything that really needs to change in your life in order for you to live a fulfilled life in Jesus Christ? Are you willing to commit to 760 attempts to achieve successful and lasting change?

No matter how many times you have tried to change in the past, will you consider trying to change one more time and allow me the privilege of guiding you along the way? If you are ready to change, I can show you the way. A Chinese proverb states, "A journey of a thousand miles begins with the first step." It is my prayer that you not only enjoy reading *Are You Ready to Change?*, but that you apply the principles you discover in it every day as a matter of practical, daily choice. I pray that these simple principles will transform your life so you will be more fulfilled, successful, and productive for the kingdom of God as you discover abundant life in Jesus Christ. Are you ready to change? Let's begin.

First, I need you to get a journal. One key to successful changers is they become great students of their own habits; they become highly self-aware and diligent to manage themselves well. Your journal will become a tool to help guide you through the change process. You will begin using it in chapter one as you read through this book. Make entries regarding key passages that resonate with you. Read over and memorize the passages that mean the most to you. Your writing will tell you how you feel about what you are thinking. You will develop an awareness of patterns in your daily environment that either enhance your ability to change or cause you to stumble.

You can journal a note from your daily Bible study. You can write about a significant event, positive or negative, from the events of your day. You can record a victory over temptation. You can record the events and key elements of a failure to prepare for a future victory. Your journal becomes a tool with data to manage your life choices. In essence, you become your own social scientist by studying your own habits and behaviors. A host of credible, scientific studies prove a direct correlation between journal writing and successful behavior change. The apostle Paul encouraged this exercise in mindfulness when he wrote, "For the weapons of our warfare are not carnal but mighty in God for pulling down strongholds, casting down arguments and every high thing that exalts itself against the knowledge of God, bringing every thought into captivity to the obedience of Christ" (2 Cor. 10:4–5).

Second, think about what you want to change and why you want to make this particular change. The most effective reason for making life changes as a Christian is to fulfill the purpose of your creation, bringing pleasure to your heavenly Father, and fulfilling the plan and purpose He has for your life. Again, we read this from the apostle Paul: "For we are His workmanship, created in Christ Jesus for good works, which God has prepared beforehand that we should walk in them" (Eph. 2:10). God created you with a specific plan and purpose in His mind. You are not a failure. You are His poem, His handiwork—and your heavenly Father does not create junk. What He has for you in this life is already prepared, finished, and completed. All you have to do is discover it and get busy fulfilling it. We will learn more about how to discover our purpose in chapter four. Focus and disciplined action on a single, vital behavior change will dramatically transform your life. You must be passionate about the change, and you must be disciplined to continue in the change to make it a new, permanent, positive, productive habit.

Third, you need to e-mail me (michael@ruready2change.com) and let me know that you have decided to make this journey with me. I will provide you with prayer support that will connect you to an entire network of "change agents" who provide constant support and encouragement. These are people who started out right where you are at this very moment. They are further down the road than you are, and they can help guide you along the way to your successful change as well. Change is not a "one and done" kind of event. Change is constant and dynamic, a process that requires vigilant attention. E-mail me about your intention to read and apply the information in this book, and let's get started. Are you ready to change?

CHAPTER 1

Are You Ready to Change?

> Moreover the LORD your God will circumcise your heart and
> the heart of your descendants, to love the LORD your God with
> all your heart and with all your soul, so that you may live.
> —Deuteronomy 30:6

> To change a habit, make a conscious decision,
> then act out the new behavior.
> —Maxwell Maltz

Take a good look around you. From one country to another we see evidence of a world in chaos. Even in our own country, which espouses the credo that "all men are created equal," we see a continuing stream of injustices. Moving from the ideal to daily reality remains a constant challenge in the transformation of the human heart. From one end of the social and economic spectrum to the other, between polarized points of view regarding human virtues and values, we see evidence of the constant stream of people's inner pain.

Far too often this persistent pain results in hopelessness and despair that lead to chronic and debilitating mental illness and that final act of desperation, suicide. Millionaire rock stars, Wall Street superstars, Hollywood celebrities, middle-aged homemakers, disillusioned teenagers, and military veterans—none of them seem to be immune from the consequences of a toxic cocktail of painful life events, fractured dreams, empty promises, betrayal of authority figures, distorted thinking, damaged emotions, and the consequences of ineffective and harmful life choices.

The good news is that life does not have to be lived this way or end this way. Get this point, and get it now: if you are capable and willing to change what you think, what you believe, and how you behave, you can influence and change the circumstances of your life. If you are willing to do these things, you can live in the words of Jesus Christ: "I have come to give you life and that life more abundantly." Your life is the sum of what *you* believe to be true about *you*. You cannot change anything about your life or accomplish any of your dreams, goals, and desires until you fundamentally change what you believe to be true about you. Why believe a lie about who you are and what you were created to become, when you can begin to believe the truth about who you are and the purpose for which your heavenly Father created you?

> Your life is the sum of what *you* believe to be true about *you*.
> You cannot change anything about your life or accomplish any
> of your dreams, goals, and desires until you fundamentally
> change what you believe to be true about you.

There is an old adage that says, "When the student is ready, the teacher arrives." Pain and adversity seem to motivate a large number of people to the point where they can decide to live a different life. Very simply, pain becomes a motivator for change. Conversely, this same pain and adversity may cripple some people, who then become so accustomed to the dysfunction of their lives that it becomes the new "normal." Over time it becomes very difficult for them to believe that they can live a life other than one of constant hopelessness and despair.

Consequently, change—even change we want—coupled with dissatisfaction over our current position in life, can be insufficient to propel us—to propel *you*—into significant changes in thinking that will drive different behaviors and associated outcomes in life.

In her book, *Choose the Happiness Habit*, Pam Golden demonstrates contrasting perspectives on pain and adversity. "Take the story of two brothers who are twins. One grows up to be an alcoholic bum. The other becomes an extremely successful businessman. When the alcoholic is asked why he became a drunk, he replies, 'My father was a drunk.' When the successful businessman is asked why he became successful, he replies, 'My father was a drunk.'"

Adversity in the form of challenging life events comes to all of us. The quality of a person's life correlates directly to the way that person chooses to respond to those life events. When adversity is self-inflicted, we need to learn to stop choosing poorly. When adversity comes from the changing elements of life beyond our control, we still need to respond in a way that improves the outcome rather than adding to the destructive elements inherent to all of life's major challenges.

Your pathway to finding peace and contentment in life begins with your own willingness to change. Accepting Jesus Christ as the Lord and Savior of your life does not automatically cause you to be fruitful and live as an effective Christian in our current modern world. The apostle Paul wrote, "I, therefore, a prisoner for the Lord, beg you to lead a life worthy of the calling for which you have been called" (Eph. 4:1). We cannot "lead a life worthy"—or change anything in life—without first changing the root cause of our current condition: our thinking.

Have you ever seen the toy called Newton's Cradle that demonstrates Isaac Newton's third law of motion: that every action has an equal and opposite reaction? It consists of five steel balls suspended side by side, touching each other. You pull one ball away from the others and release it, and when it swings back into place, it compels the ball at the opposite end to swing outward. If you pull two adjacent balls to the side and release them together, they compel two balls at the opposite end of the line to respond. Every action has an equal and corresponding reaction.

Our thoughts operate in the non-physical world in a similar cause and effect relationship. Negative thoughts create negative outcomes, and positive thoughts create positive outcomes. James Allen uses a farming metaphor to illustrate this point. You plant corn and you harvest corn. You plant peas and you harvest peas. The idea of changing ourselves can be very disturbing and unsettling, but so are the consequences of failing to change. You sow negative thoughts, and you reap negative behavior and consequences. Positive begets positive and negative begets negative. Tragically, people bemoan the consequences of their negative thinking and choices, all while feeding the cause. Are you ready to change?

> Our pathway to finding peace and contentment in life begins with our own willingness to change. We cannot change anything in life without first changing the root cause of our current condition: our thinking.

The Change Process

Everything you need to become a new you, and everything you need to learn to change and improve the quality of your life, is readily available in the world around you. A massive amount of information relevant to making significant life changes is accessible to you. New advances in the understanding of the human brain emerge practically every day as the field of neuroscience grows and develops. Things we are learning about the human brain are quickly manifesting into purposeful and intentional teaching and coaching programs. This new knowledge can equip you with the information and skill development to maximize your talents and abilities to live life to your full potential. *If* you manifest personal motivation, *if* you come to the point where you are dissatisfied with the quality of your life in the status quo, and *if* you are willing to accept total responsibility and accountability for what you think, what you believe, and how you behave, a new life awaits you.

Using biblical truth, orthodoxy, and fundamental theology, and coupling it with physiological truth—evidence-based neuroscience about how our heavenly Father created our brains—we can construct a purposeful model for creating and managing change in our lives, which will result in a fruitful and abundant life in Jesus Christ. The apostle Paul wrote, "Therefore if any man be in Christ, he is a new creature: old things are passed away; behold, all things are become new" (2 Cor. 5:17). The work of a new creation in you is even greater than God's work of creating the world. British pastor Charles H. Spurgeon wrote of this miraculous change in sermon 881, delivered July 18, 1869:

> My brethren, it was more difficult, if such terms are ever applicable to Omnipotence, it was more difficult to create a Christian than to create a world. What was there to begin with when God made the world? There was nothing; but nothing could not stand in God's way—it was at least passive. But, my brethren, in our hearts, while there was nothing that could help God, there was much that could and did oppose him. Our stubborn wills, our deep prejudices, our ingrained love of iniquity, all these, great God, opposed thee, and aimed at thwarting thy designs … Yes, great God, it was great to make a world, but greater to create a new creature in Jesus Christ.

Let me give you the gist and purpose of writing this book. Life is not about what has happened or is happening to you in daily life events. Living an abundant life, the life that Jesus tells us about, is in how we *choose to respond* to what has happened or is happening to us. The truth is, you can change. You can learn how to choose more effectively, more productively, in response to daily life events. You can become adaptable and resilient in managing your thoughts and actions to make your daily life choices. The way you choose to see life events—the particular perspective you take on very challenging life events—determines your state of mind and the resulting quality of your life.

If we are to truly live and fulfill the life plan our heavenly Father has for each of us, we must believe that "greater is He who is in us, than he who is in the world." We do not have to strive for victory over the flesh, the world, and the devil. We already have the victory. Victory in living an abundant life in Christ is not something we need to attain, but it is something we need to retain. The devil cannot defeat us, but we can defeat ourselves. Spiritual warfare is not in the events and circumstances of our daily lives. Spiritual warfare is in our minds. The battle is in our thinking and related behavior. Satan has no power over you or your life unless you surrender that power to him. When you can believe that you already have victory then you can begin to change and live life in that victory.

In his timeless tract, *Byways of Blessedness*, James Allen writes, "Your difficulty is not contained, primarily, in the situation which gave rise to it, but in the mental state with which you regard that situation and which you bring to bear upon it." Your perspective on a life event frames how you experience that event. Your thinking about the event will create an emotional response to the experience. Your emotions will then compel you toward an associated behavior in response to the event. All of this goes back to a cause-and-effect relationship created by the perspective (the focus frame and mental model) you bring to bear on the event.

The more positive and productive your thinking and emotions are in a purposeful, disciplined response, the more positive and productive will be the outcome. The more negative and disruptive your thinking and emotions are in a reactive, mismanaged response, the more negative and disruptive will be the outcome. This is a sowing-and-reaping principle. What you put in determines what you get out. Daily life is about the constant management of your response to events. The following illustration makes this point very clear.

> Your difficulty is not contained, primarily, in the situation which gave rise to it, but in the mental state with which you regard that situation and which you bring to bear upon it.
> —James Allen

Russell Wilson, professional quarterback for the Seattle Seahawks, was playing the worst game of his career in the 2014 NFC championship game against the Green Bay Packers. With only five minutes remaining in the game, he threw his fourth interception—the most interceptions he had ever thrown in any game in his career. How would any of us define adversity? For Russell Wilson, it could very well have been throwing four interceptions, playing the worst game of his career, and earning the lowest quarterback efficiency rating of any championship game ever played.

But life is not about what is happening to us. Rather, it is about how we choose to respond to what is happening to us. So, if you are Russell Wilson, the number of passes intercepted by the competition is not what matters most. Rather, it is the number of passes thrown for winning touchdowns that matters most. After leading an improbable and frantic comeback in the last five minutes of the game, Wilson threw the game-winning touchdown pass, propelling his team into their second consecutive Super Bowl.

Ironically, this principle was evident again in the Super Bowl between this same Seattle Seahawk team and the New England Patriots. An improbable catch by a Seahawk receiver put Seattle in position to win a second consecutive world championship. This time it was a player on the opposing team, not Russell Wilson, who managed his emotions and literally stepped up to secure the New England victory. Instead of focusing on what some were calling a "déjà vu" pass completion that had resulted in a New England defeat seven years earlier, the Patriots remained focused on the present situation, recognized the Seattle formation that indicated and telegraphed the planned play, and responded with clear and decisive execution to win the game.

Life is never about what is happening to us; it is about how we choose to respond to what is happening to us. Life is not about adversity, losing a world championship, losing a job, losing a spouse, losing a child, being the target of bigotry, or overcoming a dysfunctional family. Life is about how we respond to these events when they occur in our lives. All of us are going to make mistakes. All of us are going to stumble. All of us can expect to get knocked down in life. It is how we get back up that matters most.

Pain in life is real, but suffering is a choice. The key is in learning how to respond to events and doing so in the power of the Holy Spirit because your heavenly Father has made you to become more than a conqueror. The apostle Paul, the major contributor to the entire New Testament, was not without his trials, challenges, and difficulties in life. Yet in the midst of all his significant life events, he wrote, "I, therefore, a prisoner for the Lord, beg you to lead a life worthy of the calling to which you have been called" (Eph. 4:1). Another way of reading this passage is this: we are to *walk* worthy of our calling. Do you know why God created you? Do you have an awareness of your life's purpose? Are you connected with the gifts and talents God has given you? Are you ready to become the person God created you to be and to fulfill the plan He has for your life? Are you ready to change?

> Pain in life is real, but suffering is a choice. The key is in learning how to respond to events and doing so in the power of the Holy Spirit because your heavenly Father has made you to become more than a conqueror.

This book provides you with a template crafted from God's biblical wisdom, and the acquired knowledge and understanding of how we are "fearfully and wonderfully made" (Ps. 139:14), to transform your life and conform you—the sum total of your being—into the nature, character, and image of Jesus Christ (Rom. 8:29). Our heavenly Father, in His wisdom and power, is uniquely qualified and capable of providing us with the understanding and ability to live victoriously in this world He created. Corrupt as that world is from the sin of fallen humanity, our heavenly Father does not intend for us to just hang out, wring our hands, and cope with living life until the second coming of His Son, Jesus Christ. He intends for us—and has made it possible for us—to live with and overcome adversity, to live with and overcome the pain of life events. "Yet in all these things we are more than conquerors through Him who loved us" (Rom. 8:37).

Make no mistake about this: we live in a very challenging, threatening, and—as the psalmist would write—"tumultuous time."

However, when has this corrupt and fallen world *not* been a challenging, threatening, and tumultuous place to live? We may compound our own resistance to motivation and unwillingness to change by falsely thinking that we live in a time far worse than any other period in history. This simply is not true. All generations have always lived with the tense polarity of living life to the fullest or merely existing in slow death.

Remember this: what you get in life is what you create or what you allow in your own daily choices. You are accountable and responsible for what you think, what you believe, and how you behave. Sadly, today's social structures seem to feed and sustain for too many people the notion that they are powerless victims and passive observers of life. Others fantasize that mere attendance at a "millionaire mind-set seminar" will propel them toward living a life of material acquisition and the pleasures of this world. Both of these views are inconsistent with a biblical model of the abundant life that Jesus taught.

Creating Perspective

Once again, the good news is that somewhere between these two extreme, conflicting, polarized options is a third alternative. That option starts with acknowledging and believing in God the Father, God the Son, and God the Holy Spirit. Where you choose to begin in your thinking and beliefs ultimately guides you toward choices and their outcomes, natural consequences in cause-and-effect relationships. Change is an integral part of our lives. Adversity is a reality of living in our present world. Living life well means managing our thoughts, attitudes, and actions purposefully and intentionally. It requires constant vigilance, resilience, and willingness to adapt to changing life events. By doing so, we create healthy mental, emotional, physical, and spiritual inner harmony, as our response capacity exceeds the magnitude of these life events. The key to living in right relationship with others and with self begins by living in right relationship with God. People who live out a personal, abiding, committed relationship with Jesus Christ have the capacity to confront adversity from a perspective different from that of other people in the world. The result is a life lived to the fullest and filled with peace.

> Where you choose to begin in your thinking and beliefs ultimately guides you toward choices and their outcomes, natural consequences in cause-and-effect relationships.

The fact is that all of us are going to experience and endure adversity and terrible life events—and be deeply wounded in the process. Another fact is this: you do not have to be bound by negative memories, toxic emotions, or the disruptive, dysfunctional outcomes of those experiences. You can choose to be victorious, an overcomer who is more than a conqueror, as your life continues beyond those events. Our heavenly Father desires for us to live beyond those events and to use the pain and hurt of our lives as a means to reach into the lives of other hurting and broken people. As we will discuss later, the spiritual purpose for our physical pain and adversity, as designed by our heavenly Father, is to create empathy that moves us to compassion. We can choose to get into the pain and adversity of others who do not have a deep, abiding, personal relationship with Him.

Consequently, our heavenly Father—who loved us to the point of sacrificing His own Son, Jesus Christ—uses the pain of our lives to help us minister and serve in the lives of others, which can ultimately result in their spiritual salvation. When you gain a biblical perspective of God's purpose for the pain and adversity of your life, it becomes a means to a greater end in your life. The pain and adversity of life correct and perfect us, molding us into the nature and image of our Lord and Savior, Jesus Christ.

Why You Should Read This Book

Your heavenly Father wants you to live life and to live it abundantly. Jesus explained this concept in His own words: "Most assuredly, I say to you, I am the door of the sheep. All who ever came before Me are thieves and robbers, but the sheep did not hear them. I am the door. If anyone enters by Me, he will be saved, and will go in and out and find pasture. The thief does not come except to steal, and to kill, and to destroy. I have come that they may have life, and that they may have it more abundantly" (John 10:7–10). Your path to a victorious life of biblical abundance begins in replacing faulty, distorted, worldly thinking about life with an accurate biblical worldview.

What a great tragedy it is today to see so many people professing Christianity as the center of their worldview when they actually have no working knowledge or accurate understanding of the Holy Bible! Unfortunately, this is our current reality. The more illiterate we become in the Word of God, the less we know about how to understand the world in which we live, how to respond to the daily life events we are likely to encounter, and how to live in the fruit of the Spirit rather than walk in the ways of the flesh (Gal. 5:19–23).

Our heavenly Father is more than able and willing to make Himself known to us. In the life of Moses, we see a man in a deep, abiding, up-close-and-personal relationship with almighty God. In Psalm 16, we find King David writing of the secret to contentment and great gladness in times of tumultuous peril. David asked God to preserve him, not out of an attitude of fear, loneliness, rejection, or despair, but out of quiet confidence in his heavenly Father's ability to protect him, lead him, and even resurrect him from the dead, if necessary. Despite his current condition, David gave God the highest honor, saying, "I trust you." David submitted himself to the sovereignty of God in every aspect of his life. Are you prepared to do the same? Are you ready to change?

> The more illiterate we become in the Word of God, the less we know about how to understand the world in which we live, how to respond to the daily life events we are likely to encounter, and how to live in the fruit of the Spirit rather than walk in the ways of the flesh (Gal. 5:19–23).

CHAPTER 2

Why You Struggle to Change

Create in me a clean heart, O God, and
renew a steadfast spirit within me.
—Psalm 51:10

Everyone thinks of changing the world, but
no one thinks of changing himself.
—Leo Tolstoy

Common sense and a lot of research dictate that if you want to change the outcomes of your life and improve your performance in both your personal life and professional life, you have to learn how to manage yourself. Simply stated, you have to learn how to make more effective choices so you derive more effective outcomes and consequences from the choices you make. If your life is going to be more reflective of who you want to be and what you desire to accomplish, then it is absolutely necessary for you to learn to close the gap between what you believe to be true and what you ultimately reveal in your chosen behavior. Direct observation of human behavior, particularly among those who claim to believe in God, His Son, salvation, redemption, and a host of other biblical truths, indicates a major inconsistency between what we say we believe and how we choose to behave. Why? Why is it that within the so-called church we have such a difficult time *walking our talk*, as they say?

Authentic Christianity

Being saved does not automatically guarantee or give people the ability to live fruitful, effective, and abundant Christian lives. The apostle Paul wrote this exhortation in his letter to the Ephesians: "I, therefore, a prisoner for the Lord, beg you to lead a life worthy of the calling to which you have been called" (Eph. 4:1). Paul also wrote that in this walk with the Spirit there is power not to fulfill the lusts of the flesh (Gal. 5:16). He then went on to describe the fruit of the Spirit, which is supposed to be evident in authentic Christian conduct.

In the midst of the blessing of physical prosperity in America, we can easily be misled to believe that the abundant life in Christ is about material prosperity, material abundance, and material blessing. A careful and complete reading of the Bible will show you that the fruit of the Spirit, lived in the biblical concept, is at the heart of living an abundant life in Christ. Abundant life in Christ is not about what you have in the way of material abundance. The pursuit of wealth is a secular goal frequently obtained without a personal relationship with Jesus Christ. The abundant life of Jesus is about who you are and what you do. It is about your contentment in knowing that even when you live in abject physical poverty, "the joy of the Lord is [your] strength."

> Abundant life in Christ is not about what you have in the way of material abundance. The pursuit of wealth is a secular goal frequently obtained without a personal relationship with Jesus Christ.

The authentic Christian lives and walks in the Spirit and lives a life free from sin in the power of the Holy Spirit. Living a transformed and abundant life in Christ is more than being saved and making mental assent to biblical doctrine. Being transformed and living in spiritual abundance requires that we seek after God and the things above, that we put off the old man in the flesh and put on the new man, who is renewed (transformed) in knowledge after the image of Jesus Christ (Col. 3:1–15). The apostle Paul literally begged us to live a life worthy of God's calling. He pleaded with us in several of his letters to die to the ways of the world, live in holiness, engage in spiritual transformation, renew our minds, buffet our flesh, and run the race to win the crown of glory (Eph. 4:17–20; Rom. 8:12–13; Gal. 5:16–17; 1 Pet. 1:14–16; Rom. 12:1–2; Eph. 4:22–24; Matt. 11:28–30).

In both the gospel of Mark and the gospel of Luke, we find the parable of the soil and the seed. The seed is the Word of God, and the soil represents the human heart. Only one heart is productive and fruitful. Even in the third kind of soil, the weeds grow up to choke out the potential fruit. The weeds represent the cares of this world, the deceitfulness of riches, and the desire for other things in the world. This type of heart has no desire for the spiritual things or for the heavenly kingdom. It is a life lived in compromise, and as such it is a life lived without walking in total obedience to the Word of God.

When other people look at you, what "soil" do they see in your in life? Can other people see the changes in your character and behavior? Can the people who knew you before you made your profession of faith tell that you are different now? Can you tell that you are different in your thoughts, desires, attitudes, goals, and key motivational drivers for your life?

The apostle Peter wrote in his second epistle that unless we cultivate and make daily spiritual disciplines a part of our lives, we will live "ineffective and unfruitful in the knowledge of our Lord Jesus Christ." Every authentic Christian has an obligation to learn and practice these fundamental disciplines to live the abundant life that Jesus came to offer us all. The process of spiritual transformation is not a work of the flesh but a work produced by the power of the Holy Spirit. We can quench this power, and we can try to make ourselves over in our own image rather than the image and character of Jesus Christ. You will learn and apply these key disciplines in parts II and III as you continue your reading.

A life of spiritual transformation is not a self-help course or some extreme makeover according to the principles and practices of worldly philosophy. God has provided the means for us to be transformed into the image of His Son. The book of Titus tells us, "For the grace of God that brings salvation has appeared to all men, teaching us that denying ungodliness and worldly lusts, we should live soberly, righteously, and godly in this present world" (Titus 2:11–12). To live soberly means to manage our lives well. By cooperating with the power of the Holy Spirit, an authentic Christian is to be Spirit-disciplined and Spirit-controlled, not just self-disciplined and self-controlled.

> A life of spiritual transformation is not a self-help course or some extreme makeover according to the principles and practices of worldly philosophy (Col. 2:8). God has provided the means for us to be transformed into the image of His Son.

Authentic Christians who are living the abundant life in Christ are deeply committed and sold out to living under the authority and power of the Holy Spirit. As such they are deeply committed to pursuing excellence in Jesus and demonstrating His character, nature, conduct, and behavior in every aspect of their lives. Every day these authentic Christians seek to continually learn and grow in the development of their spiritual walk. Christ rules in their hearts, and He is their treasure. All their dreams, hopes, aspirations, passions, and ambitions are surrendered to God's will and sovereignty for their lives.

Authentic Christians who choose to live "soberly, righteously, and godly" have tremendous awareness of their strengths and weaknesses, recognizing how their habits and behavior affect the lives of both fellow believers and nonbelievers alike. They are fully aware that any lapse into sin brings reproach and shame on the name of the Lord Jesus Christ. Consequently, authentic Christians take responsibility and accountability for their thinking, attitude, and behavior. They never shift blame, make excuses, or become victims of circumstances. They live in abundance in their core beliefs, are creative in problem solving, and are committed to excellence in Christ. Like the apostle Paul, they can sing songs of praise in the middle of life's most difficult circumstances, trials, and struggles.

> Authentic Christians who choose to live "soberly, righteously, and godly" have tremendous awareness of their strengths and weaknesses, recognizing how their habits and behavior affect the lives of both fellow believers and nonbelievers alike. Authentic Christians take responsibility and accountability for their thinking, attitude, and behavior.

Why We Resist Change

A fundamental concept for a Christian to remember is that our life in Christ is going to be full of changes, and a part of us just does not want to do it. That part of us that resists being changed is what the Bible calls our flesh. Fortunately, we have the Holy Spirit to help us change once we make our profession of faith. Unfortunately, there is so much confusion over the purpose of the Holy Spirit in the life of the believer that most people are left to fend for themselves, and that explains why so many Christians struggle in their transformation process. Without the proper understanding of the Holy Spirit in your life, you are left to try to control and will yourself into a spiritual transformation using your flesh as the primary tool.

Guess what. You cannot use your flesh to achieve what your flesh is continually resisting—transformation. Even neuroscience has now begun to discover that there are physical parts of the brain that resist change. Later I will discuss how our brain physically works against our conscious effort and desire to change our habits. For now, trust me when I say that your brain takes the path of least resistance until it encounters some overwhelming and compelling need to change.

Not only do we have the Holy Spirit to help us in this matter of putting our flesh to death and leading us into spiritual maturity, but the church is also supposed to be playing a role and serving that function as well. The Bible tells us that the fundamental responsibility of a church is to equip the saints (Eph. 4:11–12). Equipping carries with it a connotation of preparing an army for battle. From my military days, I know that it takes nearly three support personnel behind the lines to support one fighter on the front line of the battlefield. Equipping is hard work, and the church must develop and organize itself as a teaching organization to fulfill this role in the life of the believer. Teaching organizations are themselves grounded in fundamental disciplines of behavior, and they must preach, teach, practice, and master these disciplines in the individual lives of their members.

> Without the proper understanding of the Holy Spirit in your life, you are left to try to control and will yourself into a spiritual transformation using your flesh as the primary tool. Guess what. You cannot use your flesh to do what your flesh is continually resisting—transformation.

Change is a dynamic that knows no organizational, geographic, ethnic, gender, or worldview boundaries. As human beings, we all have the same fundamental emotional, mental, and physical reactions and responses to change. We don't like it, and we resist it. Even when it's change we desire, we still find ourselves fighting and resisting it. We lapse back to comfortable, reactive—or at best, inactive—responses that we know will not take us closer to achieving our legitimate needs, wants, goals, and desires. Organizational expert Peter Senge may have said it best when he wrote, "People don't resist change. They resist being changed!"

By "change" I mean the fundamental aspect of *becoming* different and *behaving* in a different way, of passing from one state of existence to another. I place these two words—*becoming* and *behaving*—in this specific order, for, as you will read later, what we *do* is a fundamental byproduct of who we *are*. Hence, what we are *becoming* leads to how we will *behave*. The word that best describes this kind of change is *metamorphosis*, which is derived from both Latin and Greek words meaning "to transform." A great example to guide us in the use of this word is the monarch butterfly, which goes through metamorphosis, a transformation in four distinct developmental stages of life.

Likewise, we who call ourselves Christians also pass through what I believe to be four distinct stages of maturity in our growth in Jesus Christ. If there is a disruption of any of the four life-cycle stages in the development of the monarch butterfly, we do not see the beauty of the final and total transformation of the butterfly. So too, if you do not pass through and experience the interdependence of the four distinct stages of growth in Christ, you will not exhibit your beauty or live your life in the total transformation of your spiritual growth and development. (We will discuss these four stages in greater detail in the following chapters.)

Every day I meet people who are struggling in some very difficult life events. Working in health care, I see patients, their families, and hospital staff in physical, emotional, and spiritual distress every day. I spoke with a mom whose little six-year-old daughter had just completed her tenth surgical spine procedure and was facing at least ten more surgeries. Her daughter had nearly died twice as a result of her medical condition. This mom was wiped out. During three hours of intense conversation with me, I was able to lead her through some fundamental beliefs, helping her to change her focus, and giving her strength and encouragement from God's Word to see more clearly about how to choose her responses and frame her attitude in this life event.

What about you? Are you living your life abundantly or just trying to survive another day? Have you read other books about being positive, self-help books that read like cotton candy—great to the taste but fizzling without any permanent change taking place in your beliefs, thoughts, emotions, and behavior? What if I could show you a way to cut through all those other approaches—fad programs, behavior modification techniques, "hocus pocus, change your focus," magic wands and pixie dust, and Oprah's book of the month—to achieve a real breakthrough in behavioral change and compel you into an abundant walk in the Spirit? Are you willing to give your heavenly Father one more chance at changing you?

The Pauline Model of Behavior Change

Within the text of the New Testament, we see what I call the Pauline model for behavior change: preaching, teaching, exhorting, and reproving. We *preach* the gospel to bring people to Jesus Christ. We *teach* the gospel to grow people in the nature of Jesus Christ. We *exhort* people to get them to live in behavior that models Jesus Christ. We *reprove* people to hold them accountable for failing to conform to the character of Christ.

As the monarch caterpillar moves from stage to stage in developmental transformation, so too the young believer is *supposed* to progress through the process of spiritual development that translates into daily practical behavior. How silly would it look to see the transformed monarch butterfly crawling around in the dirt rather than taking flight? How tragic it is to see Christians who should be soaring in their relationship with Jesus Christ but who are barely able to stand. They hold on to objects to brace themselves, timid in the understanding of their freedom to fly, clutching the corrupting things of this world.

> As the monarch caterpillar moves from stage to stage in developmental transformation, so too the young believer is *supposed* to progress through the process of spiritual development that translates into daily practical behavior.

The apostle Paul pleaded with the new believers of the first-century church to be disciplined and committed to a lifelong process of physical, emotional, and spiritual transformation. He expected that his efforts to teach them the gospel would have power to transform their lives. Paul created what world-renowned leadership and learning experts today call a "sustained impact-learning program." These experts in leadership and learning development have created learning models that transcend mere conveyance of information and knowledge.

Intellectual intelligence is great for learning simple addition or the Pythagorean theorem. Unfortunately, learning to change behavior requires something more than intellectual intelligence. Change requires self-awareness and empathy and a host of other skills related to what has become known as emotional intelligence. There is a place for these skills as practical tools in the life of an authentic Christian. The key to remember is that God has a desire for you to change. God has the ability to change you. God needs your willingness and cooperation to make change happen for you.

Ideas have power to influence thinking, and thinking drives attitudes that ultimately compel behavior. Behavioral change, as it turns out, is not just the acquisition of knowledge and effective thinking. It also requires coupling various emotions to bring about a compelling drive for change. The primary objective of teaching is to impact the student's thinking, with the ultimate goal of influencing behavior somewhere along the line or within the learning system. For those of us who teach professionally, behavioral change takes place more effectively through an emotional-driven process, with people creating word pictures and mental models—"seeing," as it were, in their mind's eye. This experience—which neuroscience and learning industry experts are calling "emotional experiential memory," or EEM—creates the force of momentum that in turn changes behavior.

Real learning makes an emotional connection with you, and unless you feel the consequences of not changing to more effective habits and behaviors, you stay in the rut of ineffective comfort habits that will not lead to your abundant life in Christ. Let me demonstrate an example of EEM.

Do you remember the first politician you ever voted for in an election? Unless there was some strong emotional link to your actual voting, you most likely do not remember. Now, do you remember your first kiss? Mine was in kindergarten, and it was very memorable because of the emotional experience this event created for me. First, the little girl I kissed screamed out in horror, which created an emotional memory that even now creates a physiologic response when I recall it. Second, I remember the repercussions of the event, which created another negative emotional memory.

> Ideas have power to influence thinking, and thinking drives attitudes that ultimately compel behavior. Behavioral change, as it turns out, is not just the acquisition of knowledge and effective thinking. It also requires coupling various emotions to bring about a compelling drive for change.

Another EEM event that I remember with great clarity and emotion happened in the ninth grade. I was fortunate to make the varsity golf team as a junior high student. Doing so required that I leave class on Thursday afternoons to take the team van to our matches. Frequently, the class I had to leave early was biology. On every occasion the teacher stood me in the middle of the room and berated me to my classmates. The teacher stated that I cared more about playing golf than getting an education. He concluded that my misplaced priority would leave me ignorant and mentally impoverished. He concluded that the only thing I would be good for in life was stuffing cotton into Zippo cigarette lighters.

The problem with EEMs is that far too many of them involve hurtful memories. This recall keeps us trapped in a false sense of who we are as a person. Consequently, we can inherit many false beliefs—from life events and misguided authority figures—about who we are and about our value as human beings. One thing is certain: we can always tell what people believe to be true, not by what they say but by how they behave. How we behave will always reflect what we believe. The main reason that Christians do not change is related to what they continue to believe about themselves after they become a new creature in Jesus Christ.

In coaching people through the process of spiritual transformation, I encounter a number of people who profess to believe in Jesus Christ, having accepted His free gift of eternal life, who are completely unwilling to give up false, destructive, toxic mental models of what they believe to be true about themselves. One particular person—I will call him John—lives with an "I am a failure" opinion of himself. I gave him more than fifty Bible verses that tell him what God thinks about him and desires for his life, yet he refuses to accept that these verses are true for him. I have worked with him for over five years, with virtually no change in his spiritual growth. He curses the despised outcomes of his life while directly feeding the cause of those consequences.

So, get this point, and get it now. People who choose to see themselves as failures will inevitably find a way to fail, proving their self-fulfilling belief. There is no amount of coaching, behavior modification, plastic surgery, drugs, willpower, or good intentions that can compensate for people who choose to be victims and wallow in self-pity within the consequences and outcomes of their own making. How many false, destructive beliefs are you still carrying around with you now?

This phenomenon of self-fulfilling prophecy has come to be known as "learned helplessness." Dr. Henry Cloud uses this phrase in his book *Boundaries for Leaders*. As self-fulfilling prophecy, learned helplessness is a mental and emotional trap that keeps people locked into despair, hopelessness, and a "new normal" of mediocre achievement in their personal, professional, and—most sadly—spiritual lives. "Nobody loves me. Everybody hates me." This is the standard self-talk of those in the self-imposed prison of learned helplessness.

Consequently, the most important belief in your life is what you believe to be true about Jesus Christ. The second most important belief is what you believe to be true about you. Far too often the second belief gets in the way of the first belief. You believe that you are beyond hope, so you choose to believe that Jesus cannot save you. You believe that you have no value or worth, so how can you believe that Jesus died for you? What you believe about yourself controls every element of your life.

Sadly, most of what we believe about ourselves comes from hurtful life experiences that stay with us from early childhood. Even if we are able to repent and pray to receive Jesus Christ as personal Lord and Savior, many people remain trapped in these memories, impeding the transformation of the Spirit in their lives. When we choose to change what we believe about ourselves, we begin to change our behavior.

Once you begin to change your behavior, you will change your life. The Lord Jesus Christ desires that you live a fulfilled and abundant life in relationship with Him. This brings us to the most important truth we will explore in the next chapter: we can change!

So, get this point, and get it now. People who choose to see themselves as failures will inevitably find a way to fail, proving their self-fulfilling belief. There is no amount of coaching, behavior modification, plastic surgery, drugs, willpower, or good intentions that can compensate for people who choose to be victims and wallow in self-pity within the consequences and outcomes of their own making.

Why Christians Don't Change

The major stumbling block for so many Christians is the false belief that they cannot change. Traumatic life events at an early age imprint memories that function like a mental prison. Someone said you were a poor reader. You believed them, so you became a poor reader to prove them right. You could just as easily have become a great reader and proved them wrong. Someone said you were dumb in math, and you believed them and failed your math class. You could just as easily have chosen to be great in math and proved them wrong.

The key to becoming a new creature in Jesus Christ and living life more abundantly begins with what you fundamentally believe to be true about you. Now I do not mean an inflated ego and false sense of hyper self-love. What I mean is a realistic, honest, adequate sense of who you are, a perception that is acceptable to you and conforms to every biblical truth that reminds you that you were created in the image of God. You are a new creation (2 Cor. 5:17). You are a child of God (Rom. 8:16). You were born again to a living hope (1 Pet. 1:23). You are filled with the Holy Spirit (1 Cor. 3:16). These biblical truths are spread out all over the Bible. The problem is that you do not know them, or you personally do not believe they apply to you. The good news is that you can change what you fundamentally believe to be true about you.

In his devotional, *My Utmost for His Highest*, Oswald Chambers wrote, "We cannot do what God does and God will not do what we can do. We cannot save ourselves nor sanctify ourselves, God does that; but God will not give us good habits, He will not give us character, He will not make us walk aright. We have to do all that for ourselves, we have to work out the salvation that God has worked in."

God continues to allow us to exercise our free will, cooperating with Him in the spiritual transformation of our lives. If this were not so, then much of what the apostle Paul wrote regarding the way we once lived, our former lives, and what we can be in our resurrected life in Christ makes no logical sense. Paul told us that we have resurrection power in Jesus Christ (Phil. 3:10). I love the Greek word for power, *dunamis*, which gives us our English word for dynamite. There is a difference, however, between having power and releasing that power in our lives. A vacuum cleaner has all kinds of potential and stored power to suck up dirt. But unless we plug it in and turn it on, we are just wasting our time pushing it back and forth over a piece of soiled carpet.

The resurrection power of Jesus has disarmed and triumphed over all principalities and powers (Col. 2:15). That means that none of your past thinking and beliefs, or the current habits that are limiting your growth and maturity in your walk in the Spirit, have control over you. None of your emotions have control over you, and your thinking does not have control over you. Your past life and the choices of your past also have no control over you. The good news of this biblical truth means that you can change if you want to change. We have the personal responsibility to cooperate with God and do our part in our spiritual transformation process.

> The key to becoming a new creature in Jesus Christ and living life more abundantly begins with what you fundamentally believe to be true about you.

In summary, God desires that we change, and He has given all human beings the capacity and ability to change. Whenever I hear someone say, "I can't help myself," I kindly but assertively remind them, "Oh, yes, you can!" I will repeat what other change experts have written before me: between any stimuli and our response to those stimuli, we have the capacity to stop, think, and choose our response. We can choose to be different; we can choose to change our thinking and our habits. Some of these changes may be very hard, but they are not impossible. Your thinking and habits are acquired; you are not born with them. Since they are not innate, you have the ability to change, even though you may lack the will and desire to change. Let me say again: no one is going to force you to change, but unless you are willing to believe you can change and choose to do so, you will never walk in the full assurance and abundance of spiritual blessings that God desires to give to you. The choice is yours.

All of us grew up with difficult circumstances in our lives from time to time. We can all remember a well-meaning parent's or teacher's attempt to encourage us during these times with words like "suck it up" or "pull yourself together" or "what doesn't kill you makes you stronger." These admonishers may have meant well, but self-control, while serving some limited use as a life skill, is not sufficient for creating or sustaining long-term results in changing beliefs, thoughts, attitudes, and behaviors. No doubt you have experienced your own now long-forgotten resolutions that wilted under the pressure of stress, fatigue, or sheer unwillingness to give up what you knew to be self-defeating and self-sabotaging thinking and behavior.

> Your thinking and habits are acquired; you are not born with them. Since they are not innate, you have the ability to change, even though you may lack the will and desire to change.

When the apostle Paul encouraged believers to "walk in the Spirit," he was suggesting a lot more than merely making resolutions and demanding that we pull ourselves up by our own bootstraps. Paul indicated that there are key practical behaviors we are to practice that allow us to cooperate with the power of the Holy Spirit to drive impactful and life-sustaining change in our beliefs, thoughts, attitudes, and actions. Paul told us that in Christ we have a new character (Col. 3:12–17). He told us specifically that we are to take off our old nature—literally, in the original language, to "strip it off," like taking off a filthy set of clothes. We are then to dress again, to put on those behaviors that are of the nature and character of Christ. This requires active effort on *our* part. This requires great purpose and intentional behavior on *our* part. We are to take off the old and put on the new in Christ. EEM is self-regulation with which we create experiential memory to inform us of past experiences that propel us to wiser and more effective choices in the present.

Paul did this continually throughout his writings, reminding us of the pain of walking in darkness in our former self (Col. 3:1–11). What we did in our past caused us great pain and separation from God. But Paul has told us, now that we are in Christ, what the new self is to look, sound, think, and act like. This is the functional aspect of creating new emotional experiential memory. So now, once we do our part, the Holy Spirit can take over and do His part in the miracle metamorphosis of your life.

What I am advocating here is neither works-oriented salvation nor worldly, psychological technique. You really have to be careful not to dismiss what I am saying through a previously established bias. Let me spell it out for you as clearly as I can. We are saved by grace through faith in the finished work of the death and resurrection of Jesus Christ. What I am advocating is this: once we are saved, submission to the lordship of Jesus Christ and pursuit of living and walking in the Spirit require our commitment and dedication, our effort to pursue excellence in right living. Failing to understand this fundamental biblical truth, you are left to regress to your old thinking and habits and miss out on an abundant life in Christ that is lived in obedience and passion for the Word of God. You even risk the possibility of falling away from God's grace. We are to continue in God's goodness (Rom. 11:22) or risk being cut off. Paul wrote in 1 Thessalonians 4:1–3a: "Furthermore then we beseech you, brethren, and exhort you by the Lord Jesus, that as ye have received of us how ye ought to walk and to please God, so ye would abound more and more. For ye know what commandments we gave you by the Lord Jesus. For this is the will of God, even your sanctification."

The exhortation and encouragement of this passage is in the fact that God calls us to a holy life. In our sanctification, we are to be "set apart." We are to live our lives in accordance with God's commandments, standards, and principles, not those of the world. Paul was writing practical instruction on how God wants us to live holy lives. This holy life requires us to yield to the power of the Holy Spirit dwelling within us to control all innate fleshly desires and impulses. This is not self-control but the Spirit's control of our flesh. We have to tap into this power, release it, and—through obedience to the teaching of the gospel—avoid quenching it in our lives.

This also shows Paul's concern for the practical principles we are to live out in our lives as we cooperate with the Holy Spirit in leading, guiding, and bringing to our minds all that Jesus taught regarding a holy life. Your growth in Christ, your spiritual maturity, is never supposed to end. No matter how much you have changed from your previous life, you can continue to change and abound in more love and holiness. We have been given the Holy Spirit, who empowers the willing believer to overcome sin, to overcome previous painful life experiences, and to be victorious over destructive memories and toxic emotions. There is one primary purpose for the effort invested in all of this personal change: to please our heavenly Father. This is not to merit His love and grace. Rather, it is an expression of thanks for what He has done for us.

> What I am advocating is this: once we are saved, submission to the lordship of Jesus Christ and pursuit of living and walking in the Spirit require our commitment and dedication, our effort to pursue excellence in right living.

The Pooh Paradox

As a grandfather I have been reintroduced to the joy of bedtime stories. My daughter always loved the fictional character Winnie-the Pooh, created by A. A. Milne and named after a teddy bear owned by his son, Christopher Robin Milne. The character first appeared in book form in *Winnie-the-Pooh* (1926) and *The House at Pooh Corner* (1928). Once again I have had the pleasure of introducing this lovable bear to my grandchildren.

In the opening paragraph of *Winnie-the-Pooh*, Christopher Robin, named after Milne's son, and Pooh Bear are coming down the stairs for breakfast, with Pooh Bear bumping the back of his head on the stairs. You see, Christopher Robin has Pooh by the ankle, and every day they bump, bump, bump down the stairs. One day Pooh begins to *think* that there has to be a better way of coming down the stairs than bump, bump, bump. At the moment he is just too busy bumping his head to *think* further about it. Then he concludes with a sigh of futility that maybe there just isn't a better way of coming down the stairs, so the bump, bump, bump continues. Unfortunately, some people I know are like this. They keep coming down the stairs in the only way they know how, hoping for a better way. They keep on doing what they have always done, hoping to get a different result. What a tragedy!

Many of you are already falling prey to what I am calling "the Pooh paradox," or more technically, "unreflective thinking": a form of denial in believing that your responses to events or your ineffective habits do not matter and that there is no way to change. You remain trapped in the hope that if you keep doing what you have always done, you will get a different result. This hope has often been attributed to Albert Einstein as his definition of insanity. The fact remains, and multiple sources attest to the fact, that our habits are perfectly designed to give us the results we get, and our habits are the result of what we believe to be true.

Here is a wake-up call: all your habits and choices are formed in belief and thought before you act on them. So, if you are not finding meaning, value, and purpose in your life, you must ask yourself if your habits and choices are working for you. Are they adding meaning, value, and purpose to your life? Are they filling your heart with courage or fear? Are you living your dream or frantically seeking to wake up from a nightmare? Are you producing an abundance of fruit while walking with the Spirit in righteous living, or are you vacillating between the tensions of the fleshly desires and habits you were supposed to have died to a long time ago?

Even now, you are facing another choice. Your current habits are affecting how you are choosing to respond to what you are reading at this very moment. It does not make any difference if you believe that you have habits that are in motion. Trust me; you do. What is important is that you become aware of those habits and how they control your behavior when you are not thinking about them.

> Many of you are already falling prey to what I am calling "the Pooh paradox," or more technically, "unreflective thinking": a form of denial in believing that your responses to events or your ineffective habits do not matter and that there is no way to change.

Will you take the opportunity to learn something new or at least be reminded of something you learned in the past? Admit that you have failed to take action. Close the gap between knowing and doing, and commit to taking ownership of your beliefs and habits. Only you can change the direction of your life. Only you can decide to stop wishing for a better yesterday and start creating the reality of a better tomorrow. *Thinking* about possibilities today will open the door to *doing* impossible things in your life for the future. You should be expecting God to do great things with your life. When He does, be prepared for them, not surprised by them. Go find your Bible, and let's get on the journey together to living the extraordinary life God has planned for you to live.

Truth Tellers

The story is told of Martin Luther suffering in deep depression. It lasted for quite some time until his wife confronted him in the midst of his current behavior. It seems that she dressed in black as if preparing to attend a funeral. Martin Luther noticed her attire and asked her who had died. She simply responded, "God is dead." He admonished her for her blasphemy and asked her why she would think such a thing. She simply told her despondent husband that he was the one who had told her God had died—by his behavior.

We all need a truth teller in our lives to convey the truth about our behavior the way Luther's wife did. There is a behavioral model called the "Johari window." This behavior model reveals that there are things others know about our behavior that are unknown to us. This part of the model is called "the blind zone." We all have a set of behaviors that we simply do not see. As a result, we need feedback from a loving and caring partner to help us with what we do not see. It is far too easy for us to defend ourselves and deny what other truth tellers in our lives are trying to help us see. The fact of the matter is that we will always reveal what we really believe to be true simply by the way we behave. If you say you believe in God, when are you going to start acting like it? When are you going to change? The choice is yours—bump, bump, bump.

CHAPTER 3

How You Can Change

> I will give them a heart to know Me, for I am the LORD;
> and they will be My people, and I will be their God,
> for they will return to Me with their whole heart.
> —Jeremiah 24:7

> You must take personal responsibility. You cannot change
> the circumstances, the seasons, or the wind, but you can
> change yourself. That is something you have charge of.
> —Jim Rohn

In his devotional, *My Utmost for His Highest*, Oswald Chambers wrote: "To become one with Jesus Christ, a person must be willing not only to give up sin but also to surrender ones whole way of looking at things. Being born again by the Spirit of God means that we must first be willing to let go before we can grasp something else ... When people really see themselves as the Lord sees them, it is not the terribly offensive sins of the flesh that shock them but the awful nature of pride of their own hearts opposing Jesus Christ."

Unless we surrender our entire self to Jesus Christ, we never reach a place where we can begin transforming from a life lived in the nature of the first man, Adam, to a life lived in the Spirit of Jesus Christ. Having a desire to live in a godly manner is not enough. It is God's desire to restore us back to the original creation, into His image. His desire is for us to be holy as He is holy (1 Peter 1:16).

Facing the Truth about Change

Remember that there is no magic wand in spiritual growth. There is no magic pill you swallow to die to the lust of your flesh and deny yourself to enter into oneness of fellowship with Jesus Christ. The Holy Spirit will not impose Himself on us either, making us little obedient robots. We must live out our new life in Christ by yielding to the Holy Spirit, who will lead and guide us. To do otherwise would take away from the value of freely choosing to walk in a more excellent way in the Spirit. You choose to live in Christ and die to self. This knowledge and understanding, coupled with effective behavior that aligns with biblical truth, really identifies someone as an authentic Christian.

Do not confuse your active participation in this growth and maturation process with using your own power or doing a spiritual work in the flesh. We are saved by God's grace, and we are transformed by God's power. Our heavenly Father works the change in our hearts, our minds, and our behavior when we yield and surrender to Him. The evidence of your transformation is supposed to be visible in your behavior. The Bible calls this evidence the fruit of the Spirit (Gal. 5:22–23).

The apostle Paul contrasts this transformation character of the Spirit with the works of the flesh. When you yield your life to the Holy Spirit, you will begin to produce in your behavior the outward evidence of your spiritual transformation: love, joy, peace, patience, kindness, goodness, faithfulness, gentleness, and self-control. Contrast this list to the works of the flesh: adultery, fornication, uncleanness, morbid sexual desire, idolatry, witchcraft, hatred, wrath, strife, heresy, envy, murders, drunkenness, and wild partying. The Holy Bible says that those who are habitual in practicing the works of the flesh will not inherit the kingdom of God. Now, there are lots of important passages in the Bible, but when a passage states that when we do certain things we are not going to inherit heaven, we'd better be paying attention.

We are saved by God's grace, and we are transformed by God's power. Our heavenly Father works the change in our hearts, our minds, and our behavior when we yield and surrender to Him. The evidence of your transformation is supposed to be visible in your behavior.

The transformation process, our metamorphosis, is supposed to take us from a life lived in the flesh, with its carnal mind, to a life lived in the Spirit, with a spiritual mind. The apostle Paul wrote, "For those who live according to the flesh set their minds on the things of the flesh, but those who live according to the Spirit, the things of the Spirit" (Rom. 8:5). Gaining a biblical understanding of how the mind functions will be essential to your understanding how to break free of worldly habits that are holding you back in your spiritual development. These habits are not just holding you back from growing in Christ, but they are keeping you bound in sin. That is, they are keeping you separated from the rich, full, personal relationship you are to enjoy with your heavenly Father.

Pain as a Change Motivator

Many years ago a young youth pastor came to me for counseling. He confided that he had a lifelong addiction to pornography. I warned him of the dangers to his relationship with Jesus and to his marriage, his ministry, and his job. When I asked him to pray with me for the Holy Spirit to take this desire from his heart, he declined this invitation to set himself free from the bondage of this sin. He confided that he did not know what his life would be like without the compelling urges to fulfill this lust of his flesh with pornographic gratification. It was a sin that had been bringing comfort to his flesh for a long time. Keep in mind that he was a professing believer in Jesus Christ and was serving as a youth minister in his church.

He was unwilling to repent, to pray, to ask forgiveness. He was unwilling to allow God to change his heart and desires.

Ultimately, he was unwilling to believe what the Holy Bible says about fleeing all sexual immorality. He did not want to change, and there was nothing I could do to help him. His unwillingness to repent did cost him his ministry and his job, as he was caught using pornography at work. Consequently he went into a Christian rehabilitation center for his sin, and he is now serving as an overseas missionary. The pain of hitting bottom began his restoration, and in that we can take comfort. Sadly, he could have changed without all the pain.

The apostle Paul outlined four fundamental steps to a life reborn and renewed into the glorious image of our Lord and Savior Jesus Christ. He wrote, in conditional sentence structure, that *if* we have been raised with Christ, we are to be seeking those things that are spiritual, not the things of the flesh (Col. 3:1–11). We are to put to death "flesh thinking" and "flesh habits." We do not do that until we first have a change of heart, "for where your treasure is there your heart will be also" (Matt. 6:21).

Unless you have changed your desires from the things of this world and have made Jesus your treasure, any hope of long-lasting, sustained change in your thinking and behavior is doomed. There is not enough *self*-control or *self*-will or behavior modification for you to endure the sustained discomfort of telling yourself no to the desires of your flesh. That is why worldly thinking, so-called self-help techniques, fail to bring sustained and permanent change of behavior in the lives of Christians who lack an understanding of the spiritual transformation process. Remember that your flesh is not your friend, and you cannot do a work in the Spirit by worldly or fleshly effort.

The Power of Belief

The change process, our spiritual transformation, not only has a spiritual dimension but also a physical dimension. The components of the physical dimension exist in our brains. I am not talking about psychology but brain physiology: our physical brain with its physical properties and the way it works to integrate thought and belief and turn them into behavior. Neuroscience is a field of study that tells us how our brain works, from a physiological or mechanical perspective.

Sadly, most people are completely unaware of how their core values and beliefs affect the physical performance of their brain. In the next chapter, we are going to discuss how to form these core values and beliefs with a biblical origin, foundation, and purpose. For now you need to understand that your inner core values and beliefs drive how you behave. There is amazing power in what you believe because it ultimately influences your behavior and the outcomes and consequences of your life.

Since you currently behave the way you do based on what you believe to be true, you can change the way you behave if you are willing to change what you believe to be true. Thankfully, we have the standard for all truth in God's Word, the Holy Bible. The challenge we all face is that we have had many of our old, ineffective, toxic, false beliefs for a long time. You will find that some of those beliefs are so deeply and systemically ingrained in your brain that merely understanding the process is insufficient to change to more positive, productive, and supportive behaviors and habits.

Grasping the truth that you can change does not make the process easy. Your flesh is not going to die without putting up a fight. Remember that sin wants to control you through the influence of the flesh, the world, and the Devil. There is an unholy alliance that is actively working against your desire to know the truth, live the truth, and let the truth set you free.

> Unless you have changed your desires from the things of this world and have made Jesus your treasure, any hope of long-lasting, sustained change in your thinking and behavior is doomed.

There is good news in the truth of neuroscience. Understanding how our brain works in driving behavior lines up with the Word of

God. So, rather than live in a world of mental thought and disruptive emotions that resemble a toxic waste dump, we can renew our minds, take every thought captive, bring our flesh under submission to the Holy Spirit, and begin to live life more abundantly. Once you begin breaking this destructive cycle of faulty thinking and disruptive emotions by knowing, believing, and applying the truth of God's Word to your life, you begin to improve every area of your life: your relationships with God, family, friends, and coworkers. Ultimately, you improve how you relate to *you*.

In It to Win It

It bears repeating that what you believe to be true in your heart and in your mind drives the choices that result in your behavior. You cannot have a divided heart, one part wanting to commit to and serve the Lord Jesus, and the other part wanting to seek after the pleasures and lure of the things of the flesh. The first belief that needs to change—that you *must* change in order to have a successful heart transformation—is a shift from being a victim and playing the blame game to accepting and taking full responsibility and accountability for your own life and the choices you make. It is fundamental and absolutely essential for you to believe without a shadow of a doubt that you have the freedom and capacity of choice and that your best life in Christ is a direct result of your choosing wisely.

I have worked in health care for my entire adult life. I have served as the administrative director for surgical services in a hospital where I had direct responsibility over the open-heart surgery program. Patients with coronary artery disease face a severe medical crisis. Oftentimes this crisis is the direct result of poor life choices. Bad eating habits, excessive body weight, cigarette smoking, excessive use of drugs and alcohol, and little or no exercise are all risk factors that can lead to heart disease, which may ultimately require coronary artery bypass surgery to save a person's life.

Time and again I have witnessed families in the midst of this crisis with a family member who survives the surgical procedure and is literally given a second chance at life. These patients receive a host of education on diet, exercise, smoking cessation, and weight control. Virtually every patient expresses a deep sense of gratitude and relief at a fresh start in life. They all begin their new life with great expectations, promising to make life changes to avoid suffering the consequences of poor choices again.

Unfortunately, medical studies indicate that less than 30 percent of the patients who have open-heart surgery change their habits in a way that will make a significant difference in their overall health for the future. Many of them begin to start smoking again, and relatively few sustain their cardiovascular exercise programs. Even with appropriate education and the memory of a near-fatal medical crisis, it is a simple fact that we simply do not change behavior easily, even when it is in our own best interest to do so.

Why is it so hard for us to change our habits, even when we know that failing to change them can be the direct cause of our death, both physical and spiritual? Why is it that intelligent people can choose to behave in such irrational ways, knowing in advance that the outcomes of those choices can only lead to pain, sorrow, suffering, and tragedy in their lives? Providing you the answer to this fundamental question is precisely why I have written this book and why it can be the beginning of a real turning point in your life.

We are reaching the place now in your reading where I am about to reveal to you the mechanics of your habits and choices and how you can actually control your response to any event with the greatest opportunity for improved outcomes and blessings in your life. You must decide now that you are going to believe that change is possible, that you are capable of change, and that by doing the hard work and appropriating the power of the Holy Spirit in your life, you will ultimately improve your spiritual relationship with God and your family—that you will ultimately begin living a life of spiritual abundance, which God has intended for you all along.

The Bible is full of many promises for you. A belief that is essential for you to place in your heart is not only that you *can* change but that when you seek God with all your heart, you will find Him and you *will* change. The prophet Jeremiah wrote, "For I know the thoughts that I think toward you, says the Lord, thoughts of peace and not of evil, to give you a future and a hope. And you will seek me and find me, when you seek me with all your heart. I will be found by you declares the Lord . . ." (Jer. 29:11-14a). What a promise! Do you believe it?

The most important choice you can ever make in your life is that of surrendering to Jesus Christ as Lord of your life. The next most important choice you can make is to commit to learning and applying His Word in your life. Receiving Jesus but choosing to walk inconsistently, in and out of obedience, guarantees you a life of strife, confusion, pain, sorrow, and sadness. Remember that old Sunday school lesson: obedience gets blessings; sin gets consequences. I take it that you are reading this book because you have already made your choice for Jesus. That being the case, now is the time for you to choose to walk in the Spirit, to walk in obedience, and to walk in the abundance of the full, rich relationship with Him that you have been seeking your entire life.

Remember that change can be difficult, even when we desire it. Learning how to yield your heart and mind to the power of the Holy Spirit may be a challenge when you have had daily practice at doing your own thing for twenty, thirty, or more years. The key is that once you learn to surrender, then things will not be as hard. Ignoring your hidden flesh desires may delay the pain of dealing with past choices, but it guarantees that you will continually repeat a cycle of sin and forgiveness, which will keep you from living your abundant life in Christ.

As a teenager, my wife worked as a lifeguard at a local swimming club. She has shared with me the fundamentals of lifeguard training from time to time. The one thing I remember her telling me is that you should never swim all the way to a drowning person who is still struggling in the water. In their panic to survive, potential victims can drown themselves *and* the lifeguard. Rescue swimmers are trained to swim near struggling victims, wait for them to exhaust themselves, and then move in to begin the rescue hold and guide them back to safety.

This swimming example can serve as a metaphor for our lives with Jesus Christ. We can quench the power of the Holy Spirit by trying to save ourselves or "do it my way," as the old Frank Sinatra song suggests. We can flail away, screaming for help, but it is not until we surrender ourselves totally in mind and body that the power of the Holy Spirit can become operational in our lives. When we continually make choices that contradict what we say we believe and desire regarding our faith in Jesus Christ, it is imperative that we expose the lie that exists in our heart and mind. We must expose that carnal part of our nature that has yet to die in Christ. By exposing the darkness of these hidden beliefs, we gain the freedom to stand and walk in the light of the truth of God's Word.

In the fifth chapter of the gospel of John, we find the story of the lame man lying by the pool of Bethesda at the temple of Jerusalem. When you read it, you discover that there was a story circulating among the people that an angel would periodically come and stir up the waters, and that whoever got into the water first would be healed. The Bible says that Jesus saw the man and engaged him in conversation. He asked the man, "Do you want to be made well?" Do you find that to be an odd question for Jesus to ask this man? The man was lame and could not walk. He had hopes of getting into the pool of water, but every time the water stirred, someone else got in ahead of him.

If the question was not odd enough, the man's own response was stranger still, since he did not answer the question but instead told of his difficulty in getting into the water ahead of anyone else. Does this story remind you of anyone? If the Lord is asking you, "Do you want to be made well?," do you keep making excuses about why you are still sick? As I said previously, your heavenly Father has an important plan and purpose for your life. He did not create you to be ineffective in fulfilling the calling He has for your life.

Michael E. Frisina

What you are about to learn in the following chapters, I have been applying to my own life for a number of years. I have taught these concepts to people all over the world. What I have experienced in my own life, I have seen work effectively in the lives of many others. In my unlimited enthusiasm and optimism, I believe they will work for you too. So if you are "in it to win it," let's get started.

PART II

Knowing Yourself and Managing Yourself Well

Therefore if anyone is in Christ, he is a new
creature; the old things passed away;
behold, new things have come.
—2 Corinthians 5:17

Things alter for the worse spontaneously, if they
be not altered for the better designedly.
—Francis Bacon

Achieving Spiritual Excellence

Achieving spiritual excellence—what we have been calling the abundant life in Jesus Christ—is going to require you to do more than just read the principles outlined in each chapter of this book. You must willingly develop the *habit* of applying and practicing these principles in the *daily* events of your life. Spiritual character, values, and behavior are more important now than ever before, given the complexity of our problems, the pace of change, and the instantaneous access to information in the world we live in today.

Remember, the primary objective of this book is to provide you with practical tools that will enable you to part ways with old, ineffective, and often destructive thoughts, emotions, habits, and self-limiting behaviors. Your willingness to break with your current habits will allow you to acquire new habits where you can experience higher levels of achievement, performance outcomes, and peace of mind in your walk with Jesus Christ. You will learn tangible, reasonable, practical tools that you can apply to your thoughts, emotions, attitudes, and behavior to improve your effectiveness in all three levels of relationships—your relationship to your heavenly Father, your relationship with others, and your relationship with your "self."

Managing Your Response to Life Events

Within your personal life are *events*, the "stuff" of life that happens to us. There are events of an individual nature (like a personal medical crisis), and there are events of a community nature (like the loss of a friend). We all are confronted with events every day. This is the reality of life. In *The Success Principles: How to Get from Where You Are to Where You Want to Be*, executive coach Jack Canfield introduces an equation—$E + R = O$—to illustrate a basic idea. *Events* (E) are just things that happen, and it is the nature of our *response* (R) to them that determines the quality of the resulting *outcome* (O). The events that happen to us do not make the difference in our lives. The way we choose to *respond* (proactive response) to those events makes the difference.

Tim Kight, a leadership and behavior expert, taught this principle to the Ohio State University football team during the 2014 season pursuant to their national championship. During that season the team had to overcome several consecutive, disruptive events with injuries to key players. Managing their response to these challenging events, the team maintained their focus and ultimately claimed victory in the national championship game.

Additionally, new breakthroughs in the treatment of post-traumatic stress disorder (PTSD) are taking direct aim at mental coaching techniques called *reframing* and *refocusing*. The point is not to get a person suffering with PTSD to discount what happened to them in a very challenging life event but rather to change their perspective on the way they think about the event. The key is in getting the person to create a response to what happened in a way that allows the person to move forward in life with a more positive, supportive, and productive perspective on the future.

Behavior skills that are biblically based will help you frame the most productive responses to life and work events. While we do not have the ability to choose events, we always have the ability to choose how we respond to those events. By optimizing your response, you allow yourself the greatest opportunity for optimizing the outcomes associated with those events. The apostle Paul represents a spiritual case study in managing difficult life events within a biblical mental, emotional, and behavioral response framework. No matter what was happening to him, he was confidently able to proclaim, "And we know that all things work together for good to those who love God, to those who are the called according to *His* purpose" (Rom. 8:28).

When an event presents itself, we have the power to choose our response. We can respond to an event in many different ways. Even trying not to respond is still a response. We can be positive or negative, productive or disruptive, functional or dysfunctional. How we respond to an event is the measure of our maturity and character. Taking the event and adding our response creates the outcome. This entire process of reframing and refocusing our response to challenging life events empowers and sets at liberty the people who choose to do it. This choice establishes personal accountability for our thinking, beliefs, and actions. We own our responses, so we must choose wisely.

To help you to make the most productive choices, the next three chapters will provide the means for creating self-awareness and self-management. Chapter four will discuss the key elements of creating your core values. Physical fitness trainers focus on developing the core muscle groups as the foundation for creating a high degree of impactful physical development. So too we focus on developing a core that will maximize our behavior capacity. Rather than focus on muscle groups, we focus on key behavioral values that become our internal guide to making effective and positive life choices.

In chapters five and six, you will learn how to use your core behavior values to create a life purpose statement. Creating your life purpose statement is foundational to living life in abundance. By connecting your core values to a statement of purpose, you create the framework for personal accountability and responsibility for your thoughts, beliefs, attitude, and actions. Values, purpose, and personal accountability are the key behavioral skills to the self-awareness domain. You accept the truth of who you are in Christ, settling the issue once and for all that God has created you with worth and value. He redeemed you to have a personal relationship with Himself through the substitutional, atoning work of the blood of Jesus Christ on the cross of Calvary. He has provided you with a constant "life coach" in the presence of the Holy Spirit, who dwells within every authentic believer.

The apostle Paul turned his passion for the law into a passion for a life in Jesus Christ. To the Philippian church he wrote, "But what things were gain to me, those I counted as loss for Christ. Yea doubtless, and I count all things but loss for the excellency of the knowledge of Christ Jesus my Lord: for whom I have suffered the loss of all things, and do count them but dung, that I may win Christ" (Phil. 3:7–8). Paul was talking about a passion for living in the pursuit of perfection to the upward call in Christ Jesus. We too should have this passion to live in the pursuit of perfection, even knowing that we shall not obtain it this side of heaven. If we pursue perfection, we can discover the excellence of life walking in the Spirit.

Paul wrote, "Not as though I had already attained, either were already perfect: but I follow after if that I may apprehend that for which also I am apprehended of Christ Jesus. Brethren, I count not myself to have apprehended: but this one thing I do, forgetting those things which are behind, and reaching forth unto those things which are before; I press toward the mark of the prize of the high calling of God in Jesus Christ" (Phil. 3:12–14).

Remember that the behavioral skills in the following chapters do not change you directly. God is the author and finisher of our faith. He is the potter, and we are the clay. Just as we cannot justify ourselves for salvation—as it is the Lord who justifies us through the cross of Christ—so too it is the Lord who sanctifies us, changes us, and remakes us into the image of His Son. The following behavioral skills provide you with the means to "press toward the mark," to come into agreement with and participate in the change that the heavenly Father desires to work in all of us. God is involved in every intimate detail of our lives. He desires to use all of our life events as the training ground for our spiritual development and transformation (metamorphosis) into the image of His Son. Your transformation begins and is sustained in God's amazing and wondrous grace. We can walk in the fullness of that grace when we take personal responsibility to bring our own thinking, beliefs, attitude, and actions into agreement with that truth.

CHAPTER 4

Change Your Heart and Change Your Mind

*You cannot improve what you cannot manage,
and you cannot manage what you are blind to
in your personal habits and behavior.*
—Tim Kight

The Pursuit of Excellence

Whenever our behavior choices do not match our spiritual potential, there is a gap between how we are actually performing and what we could be achieving with the appropriate level of personal motivation and spiritual development. Performance can be illustrated by this simple formula: performance = fx (technical skill)(behavioral skill)

Performance is the product of what we are *capable of doing* (technical skill)—that is, our knowledge and training in the Word of God—multiplied by what we are *willing to do* (behavioral skill). People living in spiritual abundance are dedicated to performance excellence by maximizing their technical skill and behavioral skill. What really sets apart authentic believers as victorious overcomers in Christ is their willingness to do the things necessary in their *behavior* that most other Christians are unwilling to do.

> "If the idea of having to change ourselves makes us uncomfortable, we can remain as we are. We can choose rest over labor, entertainment over education, delusion over truth, and doubt over confidence. The choices are ours to make. But while we curse the effect, we continue to nourish the cause." —Jim Rohn

Even when difficult challenges confront them, "all in" believers remain committed to performance excellence. They find a way to optimize their performance by being intentional and purposeful in managing their behavior. That is why success or failure is never about events or our circumstances. The abundant life in Christ is always more of a factor of who we are and how we choose to respond to daily events and circumstances, not of the events and circumstances themselves. Whether you are a new Christian struggling with habit changes from your life before Jesus Christ, or you are a mature believer wondering if you will ever overcome "that sin that so easily stumbles you," there is hope for real change in the behavioral skills that start in your heart.

Your Inner Core

The first step to individual spiritual excellence is to develop and sustain a strong and effective inner core. There is no escaping the fact, no avoiding the reality that the change we desire to see in others, and our pursuit of spiritual excellence, begins within each individual. If you do not take this first step, you cannot become the believer Jesus intends, and you will lose your way to a life of spiritual abundance in Christ.

The inner core of a person is comprised of a chain reaction of cause-and-effect relationships between what that person thinks, what he chooses to believe, and how the brain chemically responds to these thoughts and beliefs. This simple yet profound principle has been stated by many wise people over the ages, but perhaps no one said it better than King Solomon: "As a man thinks in his heart, so is he." Thought drives everything.

> "Man is made or unmade by himself. In the armory of his thoughts he forges the weapons by which he destroys himself. He also fashions the tools with which he builds for himself heavenly mansions of joy, peace, and strength. By the right choice and true application of thought, man ascends to the divine perfection." —James Allen

The strength of your inner core—your thought and belief system—is the source, the primal cause of your behavior, which directly impacts your level of spiritual performance as you seek to conform to the nature and image of Jesus Christ. A corrupt core will lead to ineffective, disruptive, and unproductive behavior. A pure core, on the other hand, will lead to effective, productive, and collaborative behavior that fuels your walk in the Spirit as you deny the lusts of the flesh.

Your core is the essence of your character. Where you are in your life at this very moment is the total product of your character. How true it appears to be that so many people seek to improve the circumstances of their lives—their lot in life—but are unwilling to change and improve themselves.

You Are What You Think

Consequently, you must know your values and live them. The core on which you build your life is your source of inner strength and courage. It also is your source of external credibility and the trust you create in relationships with other people. A strong core begins with your inner thought life, which extends outward in your behavior. The purity of your inner core and its strength of conviction determine the degree of external influence you have in the lives of others as a witness for the gospel of Jesus Christ.

The apostle Paul wrote about this specifically when he stated, "For when the Gentiles, which have not the law, do by nature the things contained in the law, these having not the law, are a law unto themselves; which show that work of the law written in their hearts, their conscience also bearing witness, and their *thoughts* the mean while accusing or excusing one another" (Rom. 2:14–15).

Consider the number of highly capable, intelligent individuals in politics, business, and nonprofit sectors who have failed. The root cause has not been their lack of talent, desire, ambition, enthusiasm, passion, agility, or other qualities. What sends these otherwise successful leaders hurtling toward the ground is poor behavior that reflects a corrupt and weak inner core. As a result, they become so insulated by their sense of self-worth and value that they lose sight of how they relate to others, and they get separated from those who can give them honest feedback to guide them back to the heart of spiritual excellence.

There is great power in knowing who you are. God the Father, as Creator, gave us a great gift in our rational capacity. As a rational being, you have the capacity to create and control your own thoughts. In this capacity you have within you the power to transform your inner core and to shape your destiny. Do not forget this simple truth: the outer conditions of your life will always be found to be in harmony with your inner state. Your external state of circumstances is framed by your inner state of thoughts and values. Pure thoughts and pure values can never produce bad results and circumstances. Similarly, corrupt thoughts and corrupt values can never produce good results and good circumstances. We really do reap what we sow. Consequently, if we live in the Spirit, we should be walking in the Spirit. The starting point is what is inside your heart.

> Pure thoughts and pure values can never produce bad results and circumstances. Similarly, corrupt thoughts and corrupt values can never produce good results and good circumstances.

The Law of the Harvest: Sowing and Reaping

Who you are determines what you do. Who we are *becoming* in Christ always precedes what we *do* for Christ. The thoughts and values of your inner core drive your external behaviors. That is why we are always known to others by our behavior. Remember this: *no one's behavior is a secret.* Thought, character, and behavior are inextricably linked in a cause-and-effect relationship in the law of the harvest: "What you sow you shall surely reap" (Gal. 6:7).

> "Every man is where he is by the law of his being; the thoughts which he has built into his character have brought him there, and in the arrangement of his life there is no element of chance, but all of it is the result of a law that cannot err." —James Allen

What roots do for a tree, your core belief system does for your life and work. The foundation on which you build your life provides support and nourishment for everything you do. Belief drives habits of action. Who you are determines what you do. Your roots determine your fruit. This law can be illustrated in the following physical pathway known as the "C^4 principle."

- Convicting
- Convincing
- Compelling
- Conforming

Behavior expert Jim Rohn summarizes it like this: "Failure is not a single, cataclysmic event. We do not fail overnight. Failure is the inevitable result of an accumulation of poor thinking and poor choices. To put it more simply, failure is nothing more than a few errors in judgment repeated every day. Now why would someone make an error in judgment and then be so foolish as to repeat it every day? *The answer is because he or she does not think that it matters.*"

Michael E. Frisina

Mutual, Beneficial, Meaningful Purpose

A strong inner core is linked to a mutual, beneficial, and meaningful purpose. As stated earlier, the behavioral skills associated with developing an abundant life in the Spirit are integrated. A strong inner core is integrated to your purpose, your mission statement. You either live your life in self-awareness linked to purpose, or you live in a lack of awareness and simply live life by going through the proverbial motions.

The apostle Paul told us of his own spiritual development at the beginning of his Christian walk: "But when it pleased God, who separated me from my mother's womb, and called me by His grace, to reveal His Son in me, that I might preach him among the Gentiles; immediately, I conferred not with flesh and blood: neither did I go up to Jerusalem to see the apostles before me; but I went into Arabia, and returned again unto Damascus. Then after three years I went up to Jerusalem to see Peter, and abode with Him for fifteen days" (Gal. 1:15–18).

When you are self-aware, you can be purposeful and intentional about your core belief system. You actively choose the beliefs and values that are core for you, and you build your life on that foundation. You live and work in a way that is consistent; who you are on the inside reveals itself on the outside. You develop an active willpower (convicting), as your core beliefs are stronger than your impulses. As a result (convincing), you live a life of integrity (compelling) and earn the trust and respect of others. When you achieve this level of self-awareness, you can create and sustain a witness (conforming) to others around you with the purpose of accomplishing grand things and overcoming immense challenges.

Conversely, when you lack self-awareness, you live life on impulse. As a result, you change your values when it seems convenient or expedient, or when the strength of an impulse is greater than the strength of your belief system. When you lack the willpower and mental discipline to align your inner core with your outer behavior, people experience you and your behavior in an inconsistent manner. Consequently, you experience low trust in relationships, are ineffective in working with others, and ultimately lack any spiritual influence. In simple terms, you fail to be a witness for the gospel of Jesus Christ.

Remember this: repeated action produces habits, and habits reveal your character. Personal excellence is not an act; it is a habit. You are what you repeatedly do. Albert Einstein wrote, "The significant problems we face cannot be solved at the same level of thinking we were at when we created them." I would like to modify his words to read that these significant problems cannot be solved with the same level of *behavior* we were at when we created them. The good news is that we can change our behavior, and the tools for doing so are available to you. So read on.

Discover and Establish Your Inner Core

The real power of a pure inner core is the ability to bring people together to create something of greater value than any one person could have created alone. People seek meaning, value, and purpose in their lives. Spiritual influencers are keenly aware of the need to create opportunities where people are free to take personal responsibility and accountability for their own actions. Developing your inner core is the first step in your journey to an abundant life in Christ. Change is possible. What your heavenly Father desires for you is greater and more satisfying than any sin you can imagine in its false enticement to joy and happiness. You can be more than an overcomer; you can have victory over sin in your life and find peace in the grace of God, given to you through the resurrection of his Son, Jesus Christ.

Journal Exercises

You should be using your journal to make notes regarding key concepts of each chapter. Now you can use your journal to record your response to these reflective questions. Keep them as references to guide your personal growth and transformation.

1. Are you prepared to work in relationships with other people?
   - Are you regarded by others as someone who knows how to get along with other people?
   - Do you find yourself in the midst of conflict and strife, full of anxiety and worry as a regular daily occurrence?
   - Have you ever considered yourself a person who struggles with interpersonal relationships?

2. John Maxwell said, "Our ability to build and maintain healthy relationships is the single most important factor in how we get along in every area of life."
   - Have you ever taken time to consider your greatest moments of success and failure? Did you ever consider that your moments of success were relationship dependent? Did you ever consider that your failures were too?

   Greatest success

   Greatest failure

   - Have you ever considered evaluating your performance as a Christian by your level of effective relationships with other people?
   - Have you ever considered how the effectiveness of those relationships is impacting your witness for the gospel of Jesus Christ?
   - Have you ever given anyone permission to provide you feedback on the effectiveness of your behavior and its impact on your personal relationships?

- Do you find yourself isolated from others and having to "go it alone" to get things done and make things happen?

3. Create a list of your core values. My core values are integrity, compassion, and excellence. They align with my purpose as a pastor, educator, and author. I prefer that you list three values. Do not list more than five. For example: trust, compassion, integrity, honesty, excellence, fairness, etc.
   -
   -
   -

Ask yourself a few questions about your list to determine how you acquired these values.

- Why is each of these values important to me?
- Why do I want these values to be part of my core, given all the other values I could have chosen?
- If you know what's most important to you, then you probably will not have to think twice when you face a moral or ethical decision. You will make the right choice. King Solomon once said in his proverbs, "Whoever isolates himself seeks his own desires." Find an accountability partner. Let this person know that you are engaging in this journey of spiritual transformation and habit change. Invite this person on the journey with you.

Summary

1. Self-awareness and internal commitment: No change of any magnitude takes place within a person lacking self-awareness and an internal commitment to change. Use the compelling energy created in the power of conviction to create new conforming behaviors.

"Put on the new self, created after the likeness of God in true righteousness and holiness (Eph. 4:24).

2. Free will and free choice: People demonstrate that they really do have free will and choice when it comes to behavior and life choices. In Christ, old things pass away and "the new has come." When you became a Christian, something wonderful happened to you. You were transformed and renewed into the image of God. Now the choice is yours to behave in the truth that is within you (2 Cor. 5:17).

3. Commitment to truth: Telling the truth is essential for creating and sustaining trust. Passion for protecting trust by preserving a commitment to truth is inherent to a spiritually abundant life. There is a saying at the United States Military Academy at West Point that is part of the character development program: "Choose the harder right over the easier wrong." It may not always be easy to tell the truth, but in the long term, it results in far more good than does taking the easy path and damaging your witness and relationships (Col. 3:9–10).

CHAPTER 5

Change Your Mind and Change Your Beliefs

Craft a mission to the best of your ability, encapsulating the items that make your family and your team unique, and then run with it.
—Tony Dungy, professional football coach

Create Your Purpose Statement

Spiritual abundance is about making a difference in the lives of other people in your family, in your church, and at work. Your journey for personal change is a higher calling. It is a journey in which you discover and become all that your heavenly Father desires for you in the plan and purpose He has for your life. This journey takes you to an appointed rendezvous with God. Rabbi Samuel M. Silver wrote, "The greatest of all miracles is that we need not be tomorrow what we are today, but we can improve if we make use of the potential implanted in us by God."

The first step in this transformational journey is your awareness of your inner core and then living consistently from that core in your daily behavior with other people. One thing that keeps us in alignment between our inner core and outer behavior is a constant focus on our godly purpose, a focus on the potential implanted in us by God. By crafting a personal purpose statement, you can powerfully communicate your intentions and motivate yourself and others to realize an attractive and inspiring common vision of the future. This statement defines your purpose in life and the objectives you seek in order to create quality of life and to achieve the abundant life in Christ.

> "Be on a mission and stay focused. Success demands singleness of purpose." —Vince Lombardi

The Power of Focus

Executive coach, Brian Tracy believes, "A distinguishing characteristic of successful people is their ability to stay focused on their goals until their goals are accomplished." The key characteristic of people living the abundant life is their ability to focus on the purpose God has for their lives. Research of great organizations and their leaders reveals that people who live the abundant life consistently divest themselves of ego and make it nearly impossible for anyone to give them credit for their success. They always exalt God for all the good that comes into their lives.

People who live the abundant life are not uniquely talented or more gifted than other people. They do not possess more time, energy, or talent than other people. They are more focused. They know their power is greatest when it is focused. They focus on the long term, investing themselves in other people and their God-ordained calling. They are able to avoid distractions and establish priorities, avoiding the crisis management syndrome that drives less effective believers. These people simply focus their attention on what matters most at work, at home, and in their communities.

Do you have a personal mission statement? Do you have a clear focus? Have you allowed yourself to lose your passion, your dreams, and your zeal for excellence? Have you allowed yourself to see the work you do merely as a job and a paycheck, going through daily routines and motions, lacking a sense of purpose and mission? Are you settling for less than your best? If you feel like you are lacking energy and engagement in your work, you do not have to settle for being "pretty good." Your life and your work do not have to be this way. A personal mission statement defines your purpose in life and your personal concept of success and achievement. Clarifying your personal mission statement defines what you want to achieve in work, ministry, and life, expressing it in measurable goals and objectives.

At some point in your life, you had a "dream box." This box was the collection of thoughts and ideas to which you aspired. You were excited and passionate about the work you were going to do and the life you were going to live. You had goals and aspirations for what you wanted to become and what you wanted to achieve with your life. Along the way, something happened that allowed you to let your passion and desire fade. You stopped pursuing your life mission. You misplaced your "dream box." Abundant-life living is about helping you reconnect with your dreams, reignite your passion, and rediscover the greatness you were destined to achieve in your life in Christ by adding value to the lives of others.

Think about your life so far, and list the ten best things you've achieved in your journal. Perhaps you scored high on an important test or exam, played a key role on an important team, produced the best sales figures in a period, did something that made a key difference in someone else's life, or delivered a project that meant a lot for your business. Perhaps you led a child to Christ in a Sunday school class. Perhaps you went on a mission trip at home or abroad.

List these accomplishments in a well-formatted journal or on the notes page of your electronic tablet. The key is to place these "victory events" in a place where you can get to them quickly. Then spend a few minutes each week reading over this list of victories and accomplishments, enjoying the success you have already experienced in life. This exercise will help you to maintain a positive focus, to reconnect to your core values, and to fulfill your purpose in your daily life choices.

Be On a Mission

Behavioral change is essential to making substantial improvements in the outcome measures that drive personal performance excellence. Organizational expert Tim Kight writes, "The truth is that you cannot improve what you cannot manage, and you cannot manage what you are blind to in your personal habits and behavior." This level of intentional behavior change requires a radical shift in the current desire to maintain the status quo—the approach that most people take today regarding their walk with the Spirit.

Fundamentally, it requires understanding that performance is essentially about behavior, whether that behavior follows belief and thinking—which much of the early twentieth-century thought movement suggests—or whether performance is a function of emotional intelligence, positive psychology, and more recently, the outcome of positive deviance. All of these areas of study have a role to play in understanding performance and reshaping our thinking. More importantly, so does the Word of God.

After his eloquent and substantial presentation of the gospel in the first eleven chapters of his epistle to the Romans, the apostle Paul wrote in chapter twelve, "I beseech you therefore, brethren, by the mercies of God, that you present your bodies a living sacrifice, holy, acceptable unto God, which is your reasonable service. And be not conformed to this world; but be ye transformed by the renewing of your mind, that you may prove what is that good, and acceptable, and perfect, will of God" (Rom. 12:1–2).

> "The ultimate measure of a man is not where he stands in the moment of comfort and convenience, but where he stands at times of challenge and controversy." —Dr. Martin Luther King Jr.

What makes the difference for abundant-life believers is that they are willing to do the things that average people are unwilling to do. Everyone *wants* to succeed. But those who consistently *do* succeed are ordinary people who are on a mission. They are renewing their minds, keeping their thoughts on things lovely and pure, and consistently refusing to be conformed to this world. As a result, they have extraordinary levels of focus, discipline, and passion fixed on their purpose, calling, and kingdom vision.

- *Focus* is the ability to filter out distractions and direct your full attention to accomplishing a mission or fulfilling a dream. It is focused *attention*.
- *Discipline* is the ability to stay focused on what needs to be done until your mission or dream is accomplished. Discipline is the consistent doing of a thing, despite the fact that it is sometimes uncomfortable, inconvenient, or difficult. It is focused *action*.
- *Passion* is the ability to stay motivated, emotionally engaged, and tenaciously persistent in the pursuit of your mission. It is focused *emotion*.

The Attributes of Spiritual Excellence

What it takes to achieve spiritual excellence is no secret. There are basic things that people living the abundant life do to consistently achieve victory over sin in their lives. The attributes below form a system that will help you live your mission with purpose and intention. They will help you focus on *what* you want to achieve and *how* to achieve it. These attributes are the building blocks for living the abundant life.

A variety of organizations have developed training materials to assist in developing the mental discipline for performance. The list below is adapted from "The R Factor" by Tim Kight and "Mind Tools," a career development organization founded by James Manktelow. They contain biblical principles articulated by the apostle Paul in his epistles to both the Colossian and Galatian churches. Paul talked about buffeting his flesh. He told us to put on our spiritual armor, reminding us that we are in a spiritual battle. Having spent much of my adult life as a career military officer, I can deduce from Paul's writing some practical steps to waging this battle.

1. Manage your goals: the *decision* to achieve.
2. Manage your action: the *discipline* to achieve.
3. Manage your attitude: the *passion* to achieve.
4. Manage change: the *flexibility* to achieve.
5. Manage adversity: the *mental toughness* to achieve.

Manage Your Goals: The Decision to Achieve

Get focused. Define success for yourself. Decide what you want to accomplish in life and at work, and make it your mission. Be willing to identify any sin that seems to be a particular struggle for you. If you aim at nothing, you will hit it. Identify, pursue, and achieve your goals!

The first step in setting personal goals is to consider what you want to achieve in your lifetime (or at least by a significant and distant age in the future). Setting lifetime goals gives you the overall perspective that shapes all other aspects of your decision making. Then, when temptation rears itself at you, you can ask yourself this: given what I desire, and given what I am experiencing, what is the most reasonable thing for me to do? You need to have a plan to resist temptation before it comes at you. You need to be determined not to yield to it. You must be committed to the decision to achieve your spiritual destiny and not allow yourself to be sidetracked by sin.

To give a broad, balanced coverage of all important areas in your life, try to set goals in some of the following categories (or in other categories that are important to you):

1. Spiritual - What level do you want to reach in your spiritual walk, or what do you want to achieve?
2. Career - What level do you want to reach in your career, or what do you want to achieve?

3. Financial - How much do you want to earn, and by what stage? How is this related to your career goals?
4. Education - Is there any particular knowledge you want to acquire? What information and skills will you need in order to achieve other goals?
5. Family - Do you want to be a parent? If so, how are you going to be a good parent? How do you want to be seen by a partner or by members of your extended family?
6. Artistic - Do you want to achieve any artistic goals?
7. Attitude - Is any part of your mind-set holding you back? Is there any part of the way you behave that upsets you? (If so, set a goal to improve your behavior, or find a solution to the problem.)
8. Physical - Are there any athletic goals that you want to achieve, or do you want good health deep into old age? What steps are you going to take to achieve this?
9. Pleasure - How do you want to enjoy yourself? (You should ensure that some of your life is for you!)
10. Public Service - Do you want to make the world a better place? If so, how?

Be clear about what you want to accomplish. Put your goals in writing. Putting your goals in writing will help you think through what you want to achieve and why. When you put a goal in writing, you give it clarity, and you think about it more deeply. You are able to physically see the goal in written form, and you convert the goal into something real and tangible that stares back at you from the page and challenges you to make it come true.

Be committed. It takes a personal commitment, a decision, to make a true goal. Commitment is the hard work you do after you get tired of doing the hard work you have already done. Carefully consider the list of goals you have written. Are you truly committed to each goal? A goal is not something you would *like* to achieve; it is something you are *committed* to achieving. If there is a goal you are uncertain about, drop it from your list until you make the commitment.

Be specific. Goals are not merely fuzzy wishes. The more specific and detailed you are in describing a goal, the better your chances of achieving it. Being specific improves the clarity of a goal and forces you to think through what it will take to achieve it.

Set a deadline. The benefit of setting a deadline is that you fix your goal in time, not just in your mind. A deadline gives you a time target and a sense of urgency. If you want to achieve a goal, know exactly what you want to accomplish and when. A goal without a deadline is just a wish.

Make it something you can measure. Measurement is a way of keeping score. It lets you see what progress you have made and how far you have to go. It also tells you what is working and what is not working.

Establish milestones. Milestones are intermediate targets designed to keep you on track toward your goal. They help you make consistent progress over time, and they tell you where you are on the journey. The key to achieving a challenging long-term goal is achieving lots of smaller, short-term goals. We feel better when we are making progress.

> "The greatest danger for most of us is not that our aim is too high and we miss it, rather our aim is too low and we achieve it." —Michelangelo

Manage Your Action: The Discipline to Achieve

The best results are produced by those who take the most effective action. Set goals, then develop and implement an action plan for achieving your goals. Your action is the critical bridge between what you want and what you achieve. Your plan focuses attention on the specific, daily actions you must take to achieve your goals and fulfill your mission. A single act does not produce results. Sustained action over time produces results.

Be willing to pay the price. You can have almost anything if you are willing to pay for it. Your willingness to pay t[hat,] that is, your willingness to do the hard work and make the necessary sacrifices—gives you the power to achieve. Be careful of hoping for more than you are willing to work for. To make sure your goal truly motivates you, write down *why* it's valuable and important to you. Ask yourself, "If I were to share my goal with others, what would I tell them to convince them it was a worthwhile goal?" You can use this motivational value statement to help you if you start to doubt yourself or lose confidence in your willingness to do the work to actually make the goal happen.

Discipline is essential. Abundant-life believers make the decision to achieve, and they maintain the discipline to achieve. As we said earlier, discipline is the consistent doing of a thing, despite the fact that it is sometimes uncomfortable, inconvenient, or difficult. A decision that lacks discipline will quickly fade when faced with the hard work that achievement demands. It takes one level of commitment to set a goal; it takes another level of commitment to achieve it.

Beware of the Law of Diminishing Intent. The more time that passes before you take action, the greater the likelihood that you will not take action. Many people set goals but fail because they are slow to get going. They have good intentions, but they put off taking action. As a result, they never get started, and they don't achieve their goals. Do something *now* to put your goals into action.

Manage Your Attitude: The Passion to Achieve

For better or for worse, your attitude profoundly affects your performance. Unfortunately, many people cling to beliefs and attitudes that restrict rather than empower their spiritual drive. Your attitude is your frame of mind. It is your mind-set. It is the way you look at life. It is the way you choose to see events, people, and yourself. A negative attitude is the result of negative thinking. It is a lack of mental discipline. A positive attitude is the result of a proactive, disciplined way of thinking. It is intentional and purposeful.

Abundant-life believers always have a positive attitude. Their attitude is not determined by their circumstances but by the way they respond to circumstances. Spiritual abundance has less to do with position and more to do with disposition. Paul and Silas were singing in the Philippian jail. Your attitude will influence others around you. Great achievers understand that the right attitude will set the right atmosphere, which enables the right responses from others.

Your attitude is not something that happens to you. You are the architect of your frame of mind. You determine if your mind-set is positive or negative. You choose your attitude! William James said, "The greatest discovery of my generation is that a human being can alter his life by altering his attitudes of mind." Again, the apostle Paul would have called this the renewing of your mind daily.

Passion is a self-generated tool. You have the ability to motivate yourself, to concentrate on your purpose, to get yourself excited about what you do. Your attitude sets the mood for everyone around you. They get excited if you are excited. If you are fascinated, so are they. Recommendations you give to others that come from the heart have a greater impact.

Be fully engaged. Approach life every day with enthusiasm. Nothing great was ever achieved without passion. Passion is a powerful source of energy for success.

Be positive. When you focus on negative things, you de-motivate, de-energize, and discourage yourself and the people around you. When you focus on positive things, you motivate, energize, and encourage yourself and the people around you.

Be persistent. Be tenaciously persistent in the pursuit of your goals and your dream. Discipline yourself to stay emotionally engaged and positive.

Refocus and reframe when your attitude becomes negative. Don't dwell on the negative. When there is a problem, acknowledge it, and then focus on finding solutions and opportunities. Don't waste your emotional energy on being negative, disruptive, and counterproductive. "And the peace of God, which passes all understanding, shall keep your hearts and minds through Jesus Christ ... think on these things" (Phil. 4:7–8).

The words of James Allen clearly make the link between attitude and achievement. "All that a man achieves and all he fails to achieve is the direct result of his own thoughts. As he thinks, so he is as he frames the attitude that creates his circumstances. His condition is his own and not that of any one else." *There is nothing stronger than a believer with a firm direction and passion to reach his destination.* Witness the power of saints down through the ages.

Manage Change: The Flexibility to Achieve

Success requires constant adjustment. It is your responsibility to make the changes you need to make to achieve your goals. If what you're doing isn't working, change it. Doing more of what doesn't work, doesn't work. Success belongs to people who are able to manage change and adapt to new circumstances.

It's easy to think that people resist change out of sheer awkwardness and lack of vision. However, you need to recognize that change may affect some people negatively in a very real way that you may not have foreseen. For example, people who have developed expertise in (or have earned a position of respect from) the old way of doing things can see their positions severely undermined by change.

Often it is your ability to handle change and adapt that determines the quality of your life. Don't resist, resent, or complain about change; respond to it. Be flexible. Learn to adjust and make midcourse corrections as you pursue your mission and vision. A rapidly changing world deals ruthlessly with people and organizations who fail to adapt. If you think changing is tough, wait and see how difficult life and work become if you do not change!

Accept the fact that change is constant. Change, even change we desire, comes with an inherent element of disruption. This disruption stems from the need to "break with" one set of habits to "breakthrough" to a new set of more effective habits. Being stubborn or getting angry won't make undesirable change go away, but it will make change more difficult to deal with as you struggle to move forward.

Wise up and toughen up. You have a fixed amount of emotional and intellectual energy. Do not waste time and energy resisting changes you need to make to move to a higher level of spiritual performance. What changes are you resisting at this moment? Could you be resisting something that God intends for you to do? *Life is about making adjustments.* Understand that change always means giving up something. Don't be stubborn. Have the courage to let go. Success goes to those who are really good at creating alternative courses of action.

You have to work hard to make changes in your life—even changes you desire. The good news is that the change we desire begins to happen when we accept the grace of God into our lives. Grace changes everything, and anything can change with grace. Remember that your heavenly Father desires change to take place within you. There is the liberating power of the Holy Spirit within you. You must connect to it and turn it on in your life. The Holy Spirit has a purpose: to lead us and guide us into all truth. It is the Holy Spirit who gives us what we need to change so we can do what is right and avoid those old sinful desires of our past. When you plan carefully and build the proper foundation, implementing change can be much easier, and you'll improve the chances of success. If you're too impatient, and if you expect too many results too soon, your plans for change are more likely to fail.

Create a sense of urgency, recruit powerful change partners in your life, build a vision and effectively communicate it, remove obstacles, create quick wins, and build on your momentum. If you do these things, you can help make the change part of your organizational culture. That's when you can declare a true victory.

Manage Adversity: The Mental Toughness to Achieve

Adversity is an inevitable part of life. No one wants it, but everyone experiences it. Don't be surprised when there are obstacles, setbacks, and problems. Be mentally tough. Maintain your focus. In response to adversity, the critical issue is not how you feel but what needs to be done. That is where your focus must be.

In his book *QBQ: The Question behind the Question*, John G. Miller emphasizes how to manage adversity by focusing on two questions: (1) *What do I need to do?* and (2) *How do I need to behave?* These two questions help us avoid procrastinating, shifting blame, and becoming a victim of our circumstances.

Managing adversity requires you to develop a great deal of optimism. Optimists tend to see the glass as always half full, or so the saying goes. They view adversity in their lives as temporary, specific, and external—that is, not entirely their fault—as opposed to pessimists who view adversity as unchangeable, pervasive, and more personal. In the face of setbacks, challenges, or difficult jobs, pessimists are more likely to do worse than predicted and even give up, while optimists will persevere.

Optimism, therefore, is also an important component of achievement, and it is especially important in times of chaos, change, and turbulence. Those who have an optimistic outlook will roll with the punches, will be more proactive and persistent, and will not abandon hope.

So, where does optimism come from? Is it something we are born with, or is it learned? For some lucky individuals, being optimistic comes naturally. The good news is that, for those who don't have it naturally, optimism is an attitude that can be learned and practiced. Here are some strategies you can consider in your journey to becoming more optimistic, or in helping someone else who suffers from pessimism.

Avoid negative environments. If this is not realistic, make every effort to seek the company of positive individuals in your organization. Sometimes this may mean fraternizing with peers in other departments. Stay away from the professional complainer.

Celebrate your strengths. The key to high achievement and happiness is to play out your strengths, not correct your weaknesses. Focus on what you do well.

Take care of your spiritual and emotional well-being. Read inspirational material on a daily basis. This may be different for each person. Some may be inspired by daily quotations, others by reading biographies of successful people in their field. Still others may derive inspiration from reading about all the innovations that we are graced with. A useful website for this is the World Future Society (www.wfs.org), which keeps up with new inventions.

Manage or ignore what you cannot change. When faced with setbacks, identify what you can change, and proactively try to find ways to do something about it. We have often heard this advice, and it bears repeating. Be inspired by Benjamin Franklin's words: "While we may not be able to control all that happens to us, we can control what happens inside us."

Adapt your language and outlook. Consider how a simple shift in the language you use can make a difference in your outlook. Do you frequently say "yes, but …" in response to your team members' suggestions? The word *but* automatically negates anything you have said at the beginning of a sentence. A simple shift to "yes, and maybe …" makes a positive difference. Check the e-mails you have sent recently. Count the proportion of negative to positive words. It could be enlightening.

Focus outside yourself. Take time for important people in your life and on pursuits and projects that fire you up. Bertrand Russell once said that the quickest way to make ourselves miserable is to continually focus on ourselves. It was his love of mathematics that kept him going—and he was an avowed atheist. It's amazing that he discovered the biblical truth of denying self for a more balanced perspective on life, while so many believers struggle with having a positive mental outlook.

Nurture a culture of optimism when you are in charge of other people at work. Expect people to succeed. Even when they occasionally fail to achieve what they set out to do, be an encouragement to others so that they can tackle the next challenge. A simple "I know you'll do better the next time" can have a very positive effect on the performance of others.

Cultivate spontaneity. Consider putting aside all your plans once in a while to take a walk with your kids, play a game, or watch a movie. Getting out of your comfort zone by being spontaneous helps to develop your optimism muscle, as spontaneity essentially involves an expectation of having a pleasurable experience.

Consider the health benefits. If you need extra motivation for practicing optimism, consider the statistics linking optimism to greater health. There is new scientific evidence suggesting that immune systems among optimistic people are stronger than among pessimists. (See *www.nbcnews.com/optimism*.) Read Philippians 3:4–9, and look at how the apostle Paul kept his perspective and positive outlook, even in the midst of his physical trials. Note that he did this before there was neuroscience to confirm this mental and emotional practice.

Managing adversity requires resilience. Resilience is the ability to harness inner strength and respond effectively when you get knocked down by life's inevitable difficulties. Resilient, optimistic people do not dwell on setbacks. Instead they focus their attention and energy on taking action to make things better. They get knocked down, but they always get back up. As Dean Becker, the president and CEO of Adaptiv Learning Systems, a company in King of Prussia, Pennsylvania, that develops and delivers programs about resilience training, puts it, "More than education, more than experience, more than training, it is the level of resilience and optimism that will determine who succeeds and who fails."

Create Your Personal Mission Statement

Whatever your current circumstances, you will rise or fall, succeed or fail, on your ability to manage your thoughts and attitude as they frame your mission and vision. James Allen writes, "The vision you glorify in your mind, the ideal that you enthrone in your heart—this you will build your life by; this you will become."

> "No individual has any right to come into this world and go out of it without leaving behind him distinct and legitimate reasons for having passed through it." —George Washington Carver

Discovering purpose for your life, like becoming someone who makes a difference in the lives of other people, generates the conviction that propels positive behavior to higher levels of performance. We choose to focus on performance rather than success because success is subjective, while performance is objective. When you discover purpose for your life, you will also discover the conviction to live with sincerity and the willingness to pursue things that matter most in making a difference for yourself and for other people.

Without a sense of purpose, you will find yourself waking up every morning and simply meandering through life instead of living life with meaning. Conviction, having a sense of purpose and destiny fueled by the catalyst of urgency, makes for an explosive force to propel spiritual performance excellence. Conviction provides a lens to see any situation with great clarity and courage. When you can see yourself, your current situation, and your purpose with clarity, you are free to choose the most effective response to compel performance in your spiritual life to higher levels of excellence.

Journal Exercises

1. Without conviction, people rarely accomplish anything of lasting value that makes a significant difference.

   - What do you passionately believe to be true? Take a few minutes to make a list of things you believe strongly, and then try to identify *why* you believe these things so passionately.
   - What values have you internalized that drive your passion for what you believe to be true?
   - Is your current use of your time and talents aligned with what you are most passionate about? If not, why not?

2. Urgency has been described as a catalyst for creating conviction. Do you have a sense of urgency to fulfill your purpose? Do you know

how to create urgency to compel yourself to a higher level of energy, engagement, and performance enhancement to improve your walk in the Spirit?

3. Are you driven by a fear of failing rather than the urge to create from the power of passion in pursuit of excellence? If so, why?

4. Evaluate your focus. Where are you centering all your mental energy—on yourself or for the benefit of others and your organization? Complete the following exercise; it is a self-assessment on how you manage your mind-set and attitude. List the thoughts that hold you back and the thoughts that move you forward.

<u>Thoughts That Hold You Back</u>   <u>Thoughts That Move You Forward</u>

To what actions do the thoughts listed in your left-hand column lead? To what actions do the thoughts listed in your right-hand column lead? What do you think happens to your performance when you spend more time in the left column than the right column? Left-column thinking lacks focus, discipline, passion, purpose, and vision.

Evaluate your current sense of purpose and mission. Evaluate your vision. What are you hoping for in your future as you move forward with a clear sense of focus, discipline, and passion? Does your personal mission statement for your life tell you (1) who you are, (2) why you are here, (3) what you are about, (4) and what you hope to achieve in your lifetime?

Summary

Abundant-life believers live a daily discipline of renewing their minds. They embrace virtually every life event and become flexible and adaptable to those events to maximize their performance. Every day they live intentionally, putting their minds on things of great importance to maintain their focus. Deliberate and disciplined action to renew one's mind and improve one's behavior requires a good dose of courage.

Your behavior is the product of three factors: (1) *vision*, or how you choose to look at the world around you and interpret events that impact your life, (2) *expectations*, or what you choose to believe is true about the world in which you live, and (3) *emotions*, or the energy released from the feelings that are generated by your vision and expectations. Becoming convinced of a truth and acting on that truth consistently, day in and day out, requires mental toughness, and mental toughness is acquired through self-discipline.

Mental toughness is a hallmark character trait of high-level performers. Mental toughness is rooted in the power of being convinced about a nonnegotiable truth. It is a mental edge that enables you to perform at high levels during times of stress, fatigue, and moments that require you to perform at your absolute best. Mental toughness is the acquired ability to be more determined, more resilient, more focused, and more emotionally controlled under pressure.

CHAPTER 6

Change Your Beliefs and Change Your Behavior

> You must take personal responsibility. You cannot
> change the circumstances, the seasons,
> or the wind, but you can change yourself. That
> is something you have charge of.
> —Jim Rohn

In every situation, abundant-life believers take full responsibility for the quality of the results and the overall outcomes of their thoughts, beliefs, emotions, and behavior. Taking responsibility means being accountable for your choices and recognizing that your attitude and actions make a difference.

Though some very well-meaning people tend to deny that human beings have free will, it is inconceivable to believe in God's justice, mercy, and grace if free will does not exist. The apostle Paul wrote that we can choose to live in our sinful nature, to set our minds on natural desires and affections that do not edify us in our walk to spiritual perfection. We can also choose to set our minds on the things of the Spirit (Rom. 8:5). The apostle Peter told us to abstain from the passions of the flesh (1 Pet. 2:11). These things—setting our minds and choosing to abstain—are what we are free to do in our own will. The key question we must ask is this: am I ready to take accountability and responsibility for my choices?

James Manktelow borrows from the Hippocratic oath when he writes the following:

> "I swear by Apollo" ... So starts the Oath of Hippocrates, an oath of ethical, professional behavior sworn by all new physicians—a promise to practice good medicine to the best of their ability, for the good of their patients. It essentially boils down to a commitment to 'do no harm.' Wouldn't it be great to have such an oath for leaders—an oath of personal accountability, not just for business outcomes and for leading others, but for *leading oneself*. I am reminded of the proverb "Physician, heal thyself," suggesting that one should take care of one's own faults first before correcting the faults of others—so I add to the above: *Leader, lead thyself.*

To this quotation I would like to add, as the apostle Paul would say, "Dear Christian, I beseech you, I beg you, I urge you with deep pleading to take responsibility for your life as a called-out one in Jesus Christ."

Abundant-life believers demonstrate vital strengths that ensure their success: the drive to achieve results, the ability to accept personal responsibility for those results, taking ownership of self (thoughts, emotions, attitudes, and behaviors), cultivating collaboration and building highly effective relationships with other believers, and finally, the ability to connect with people continually in spiritual change and growth known as sanctification, the process of perfection in the nature and character of Jesus Christ.

Taking ownership of self means being aware and choosing effective responses to the circumstances and challenges of life we face daily. Change is not a one-time event. You must make a daily commitment to repentance and change every day. You are either moving forward or backward. There is no holding a middle ground in metamorphosing a life lived in the flesh to a life of walking in the Spirit.

People who accept responsibility and take ownership of self do not shift blame to others for poor results and outcomes. They do not procrastinate; rather they move to take action efficiently and effectively. They never make excuses or play the role of victim in difficult situations. Instead, abundant-life believers approach life with what John G. Miller describes as the "question behind the question": What can I do to make a difference? How can I contribute to a better outcome?

In Miller's approach, taking responsibility goes beyond merely accepting blame. An abundant-life believer who asks "what" and "how" questions is moving toward resolving problems, creating opportunities, and managing events with a positive response in order to create the most optimal outcomes out of the worst situations. They are dying to self every day, committing to a life of obedience in Jesus Christ. While this is an important dimension of spiritual development, it is easy to slip when it comes to accountability for our own behavior. This can happen even to long-term, committed believers who lose their focus on any given day, or who choose to isolate themselves, forgetting "to take heed lest they think they stand."

Leveraging Responsibility and Self-Ownership

The key to creating and sustaining a life of excellence in Christ begins with breakthroughs in individual thoughts and behavior. How we choose to see a problem *is* always the real problem. How we choose to see something, our perspective and perception, has been greatly influenced by our life experiences. We need to understand that we do not always see things in their complete context or with unbiased objectivity.

Responsibility and self-ownership function as the lever that activates thoughtful, effective action. When you take responsibility, you create quality of life and work in response to events and circumstances, change your behavior patterns, and commit to continuous learning and growth. The result is a life lived to your full potential. It is unrealistic—and even a bit foolish—to think you can improve your life if are you unwilling to take responsibility for your attitude and actions.

> A person cannot directly choose his circumstances, but he can choose his thoughts, and so directly, yet surely, shape his circumstances.
> —James Allen

A major weakness of our current society is the growing aspect of victimization. People choose to see themselves as victims of their circumstances and thereby fail to accept responsibility and ownership of self in their circumstances. There is no sin, says the prevailing thought of worldly wisdom. Sin has now become a disease or illness that needs treatment, not redemption. Consequently, the more people yield power to their circumstances and temptations, the worse those circumstances and temptations become.

There is no satisfying the lusts of the flesh. Your flesh is not your friend. If changing from a life of sin and death to a life lived in the abundance of Christ was possible through self-help techniques, then Jesus would never have had to die on the cross at Calvary. Redeeming sinful human nature was a monumental task that called for monumental action in the death and resurrection of Jesus Christ. Consequently, trust, faith, repentance, and obedience are daily requirements.

Taking responsibility and ownership for self begins by taking control of our thoughts, managing our emotions, and acknowledging the truth of our current reality and the truth of God's Word so we can move forward in creating a new reality in our lives. Remember this: *your choices, not your circumstances, define what kind of person you are and who you will become.* These choices become a battle of daily spiritual warfare. So the apostle Peter warned us, "Be sober-minded; be watchful. Your adversary the devil prowls around like a roaring lion, seeking someone to devour. Resist him, firm in your faith, knowing that the same kinds of suffering are being experienced by your brotherhood throughout the world" (1 Pet. 5:8–9).

We need to be willing to take a good look inside ourselves and become aware of the thinking, patterns, and habits that are responsible for our current level of spiritual development. The key is in finding our natural behavioral strengths, aligning them to Bible-centered core values, and then using them to create a higher level of thinking that propels us toward a higher level of spiritual performance. In the process of maintaining this alignment, we take responsibility and true ownership of ourselves. In this process, we discover true joy and meaningful purpose in life. In this process, we discover a life more spiritually abundant in Christ Jesus.

Point of the Spear

Life is about choices. We mistakenly think life is about events. No event appears in your life without some cause. The important thing to remember is that you are not defined by events. The way you choose to respond to events defines who you are. Every day you make choices about how to respond to the events and situations you experience. Really important life events are lived at the point of the spear—defining moments of truth, as some writers refer to them. You find yourself in a circumstance that you must respond to without the help of others. And the choices you make at that moment in such events define the direction of your life.

As life goes on day by day, challenging and difficult events will continually come into our lives. These challenges will require ever greater responses to gain the most optimal outcomes. The most challenging events of life often occur during times of significant change, crisis, or opportunity, and they require nonstandard responses. These are times when you must call upon your deepest capabilities and courage and go beyond your normal limits in order to respond effectively.

Change and chaos are constant in the rapid pace-, knowledge-, and technology-driven climate we live in today. There is another constant at play in this climate as well—namely, the way human beings tend to respond to the change, chaos, and stress. Change is inevitable, and so, it would seem, is our resistance to it. Yet in the midst of this climate of change, chaos, and resistance to change, influential leaders and their organizations continue to thrive, grow, and sustain a high level of performance excellence. There is hope in Jesus Christ. Paul said, "Let us not grow weary of doing good, for in due season we will reap, if we do not give up" (Gal. 6:9). There is always hope in Christ.

A young youth minister confessed his pornography addiction to his senior pastor. Confronted by his guilt, he was unwilling to pray to ask forgiveness or to ask God to help change the desires that had started early in his teen years. When asked why he would not pray, he said he did not know what life would be like without the gratification of his sin. This choice cost him his job and nearly cost him his marriage—but for the devotion and commitment of a loving and forgiving wife. He eventually went into a Christian addiction rehab program and restored his relationship with God and with his family.

Change is possible when we accept responsibility for our actions. There may be an ideal of sinless perfection for believers, but the great Charles Spurgeon and others concede that this life is quite the challenge. Perhaps that is why the apostle John encouraged us toward constant confession and repentance: "If we say we have no sin, we deceive ourselves, and the truth is not in us" (1 John 1:8).

Therefore, do not be surprised at the challenging events of life. Your life, at times, is going to be full of unpredictable and undesirable change and adversity. Be prepared for it. We have the power of choice to live a life of meaning and purpose. Circumstances cannot make this distinction for us. So do not make a difficult situation worse by responding poorly! As an alternative, consider the following options:

1. Are you open to the daily accountability of your spouse, children, or spiritual partner? Do you possess the humility to receive feedback on how you are behaving in your marriage, as a parent, or within the fellowship of your church?

2. At the end of each day—for example, when you clear your desk before you head home—take a few minutes to mentally review your day. Think about significant conversations you had throughout the day, meetings you attended, e-mails you sent, and other actions you undertook. Are you satisfied with your spiritual performance? Could you have done better? This exercise will inspire you to plan your next day around your highest purpose. Getting into this habit of daily introspection will pay dividends in the long run.

   Finally, find one or two key spiritual brethren and ask them to respond to this question: "On a scale of one to ten, how was I today as your spouse, parent, or fellow brother or sister in Christ?" If you get any answer other than a ten, ask them to tell you one thing you could have done differently to rate a ten. This simple accountability tool will do wonders at building your influence with others, focusing on change as a lifelong habit, and renewing a righteous spirit within you.

3. Decide to hold yourself accountable for developing others in their spiritual walk. Far too many believers are withholding participation in spiritual activities. We waste far too much time and money on the things of this world when we should be focusing on the spiritual development of believers at all ages. By mentoring a protégé to enhance his or her personal and spiritual growth, you strengthen your own skills and reinforce your determination to be self-accountable as you become the model Christian. Remember that the apostle Paul encouraged believers to copy and mimic him in his own spiritual walk. You should be walking diligently so as to encourage others to copy you as well.

4. When something goes wrong, look inward for solutions, with the Spirit leading you to all spiritual wisdom and spiritual truth. Remember that the difficult, most challenging events challenge our response and our self-accountability. Martin Luther King Jr. said it poignantly: "The ultimate measure of a man is not where he stands

in moments of comfort and convenience, but where he stands at times of challenge and controversy."
5. Moliere, the seventeenth-century French dramatist, said, "It is not only what we do, but also what we do not do, for which we are accountable." Is there anything that you are avoiding doing that needs to be done? For example, are you putting off a difficult conversation? Are you delaying any important decisions? Are you delegating or shifting blame for responsibilities that should stay under your control?

Self-accountability, then, means staying true to our core values despite difficult circumstances. It means doing the right thing, even when we are tempted to bend a few rules for expediency's sake. It is also the best antidote to feeling victimized by circumstances. It frees up precious creative energy for us to accomplish what really matters most to us. Above all, it entails owning up to the consequences of our decisions and choices because there is no choice without accountability.

A Positive Mental Model

> You live with your thoughts so be careful what they are.
> —Eva Harrington

Our habits are part of a cause-and-effect relationship between what we believe to be true about the world around us and the coinciding mental models and patterns our brains create to align with those beliefs. Taking responsibility and ownership of self requires a constant reexamination of these thoughts and beliefs to ensure that we are operating with the most effective mental models possible for high-performing spiritual behavior.

As you read this book and put its principles into practice, you will have moments of both victory and failure. Do not give up, not this time. This time, continue to commit yourself to permanent change. Use your journal to determine your trends based on certain situations, persons, types of sin, or other contexts when you are most likely to fail. You must become your own "spiritual scientist," so to speak, to study and analyze your moments of success and failure. Keep coming back to the cross of Christ as your starting point. Keep looking to the Holy Spirit to teach, lead, and guide you to a higher level of spiritual success. Remove from your life any object that sets you up for failure. This might mean cutting off old friendships or getting rid of your cable or satellite TV. It might mean not being on the computer alone and keeping your Internet access in an "open zone" so anyone can monitor it at any time.

The apostle Paul said to cut off, throw off, put off, and kill anything that could excite and provoke sinful desires in our lives. You need to be willing to take such desperate action in obedience to the Word of God in your life to achieve spiritual breakthroughs that propel you to an abundant life in Christ. Failure was not an option in saving the Apollo 13 astronauts, and it is not an option in saving souls either.

How we view adversity and stress strongly affects how we succeed, and this is why having a positive, resilient mental model is so important. We cannot *improve* our spiritual behavior and performance unless we are *managing* our spiritual behavior and performance. We cannot manage what we are not aware of within our own mental models and behavioral habits. This is why the apostle Paul said that we must renew our minds. Hence, sustainable, personal change to drive high spiritual behavior requires (1) recognizing our habits, (2) understanding how those habits impact and affect people around us, and (3) taking consistent, deliberate, and disciplined actions to change and improve.

The secular research of Jim Rohn, Jack Canfield, and other thought experts have a biblical basis that reveals a distinguishing characteristic of consistently successful people: they all have the ability to maintain a positive and proactive attitude, regardless of the challenge of significant life events. It turns out that highly effective secular people *think* differently from less effective people. Their thinking and operating mental models have biblical characteristics. They are:

- Deliberate
- Disciplined
- Intentional
- Focused
- Engaged
- Thoughtful

The positive mind-set of an abundant-life believer sees and acknowledges the discomfort and difficulties of a challenging situation but is constantly looking for solutions and opportunities to obtain the most optimal outcome. The mind-set of an abundant-life believer finds and focuses on the opportunity within the problem.

In spite of struggling with "failure" throughout his entire working life, Thomas Edison never let it get the best of him. All of these failures, which are reported to be in the tens of thousands, simply showed him how *not* to invent something. His ability to manage a positive mental model gave the world some of the most amazing inventions of the early twentieth century, such as the phonograph, the telegraph, and the motion picture.

It's hard to imagine what our world would be like if Edison had given up after his first few failures. His inspiring story forces us to look at our own lives. Do we have the resilience we need to overcome our challenges?

It is also hard to imagine what our world would be like if the apostles—Peter, James, John, Paul, and the others—had given up in the face of their adversity. Do we press on to that upward call in Christ Jesus? Or do we let our failures derail our dreams and the plan and purpose Christ has for our lives? And what could we accomplish if we had the strength not to give up?

Stop here for a moment and think how you feel about and typically respond to change and adversity. Make a list in your journal of your key feelings about change. Take a look at the list, and ask yourself if you see a list that reflects positive emotion or negative emotion. If you are allowing your thinking to be affected by negativity, can you see how it impacts your ability to form a positive mental model? It is very easy to give away responsibility and ownership of self during difficult events.

The good news is that taking responsibility and ownership of self is habit-forming. You can actually create physical pathways in your brain to help you make more positive, effective choices. Once activated, there are chemicals in your brain that God created—neurochemicals—that can assist you to reverse the negative, destructive process that your brain has adopted in your current mental model.

The more you discipline yourself to approach things with a positive mind-set, the more that proactive habit will shape the way you think and respond to the circumstances of life and work. Change is a process that you must engage and embrace with a strong sense of commitment and determination.

Here is a thought tool that performance experts advocate. These questions will help you create and sustain a positive mental model, particularly when you are in the middle of challenging events.

- Given the *outcome* I want and the *event* I am experiencing, what *response* on my part would be most effective?
- Am I clear about what I really desire, the goal I am pursuing?
- Do I see the situation with clarity, perspective, and a clear frame of reference?
- What are my options for taking effective action?

No More Excuses

Before any real behavioral change can take place in our lives, we must come to the point of being mentally convinced that change is real, possible, and holds the promise of better, more enhanced, improved outcomes. The simple truth is that you are not bound by any sin, worry, doubt, fear, or anxiety that the power of the Holy Spirit cannot help you overcome when you choose to change.

Abundant-life believers live in a constancy of purpose fueled by having settled the issue on the matter of change. They are absolutely assured that change is possible, good, and necessary, and they constantly bring their thinking into agreement with this truth, which is evident in their daily behavior. Consequently, abundant-life believers replace fear and doubt with optimism and assurance. Resentment and frustration are replaced with enthusiasm and motivation. By choosing to focus on the positive aspects of change—even change that is extremely difficult—abundant-life believers create positive emotions that propel them and their families and friends to higher levels of spiritual performance excellence.

Choosing to avoid the excuse trap provides us the ability to adapt and bounce back when things don't go as planned. Abundant-life believers don't wallow in or dwell on failures; they acknowledge the situation, learn from their mistakes, seek forgiveness, and then move forward. According to the research of leading psychologist Susan Kobasa, three elements are essential to avoiding the excuse trap, and they have spiritual value. Even the world can find biblical truth, even though they do not acknowledge its source when they are looking for it.

1. Challenge - When people are accountable to self and others, they view a difficulty as a challenge, not as a paralyzing event. They look at their failures and mistakes as lessons to be learned from, and as opportunities for growth. They don't view them as a negative reflection on their abilities or self-worth.
2. Commitment - Accountable people are committed to their lives and their goals, and they have a compelling reason to get out of bed in the morning. Commitment isn't just restricted to their work; they commit to their relationships, friendships, the causes they care about, and their religious or spiritual beliefs.
3. Personal control - Accountable people spend their time and energy focusing on what they can control: their responses to events. Since they put their efforts where they can have the most impact, they feel empowered and confident. Those who spend time worrying about

uncontrollable events can often feel lost, helpless, and powerless to take action.

The mind-set or thinking model that contrasts that of responsibility and ownership of self is a mental model of blame-shifting and excuse-making. Far too often, struggling believers fall into the trap of accepting excuses for average or low-level spiritual growth rather than taking initiative to solve the problems that are at the root of their poor performance. These individuals sadly become very adept at finding ways to cope with problems rather than solving them. This excuse mentality has a way of screening out all evidence of responsibility, accountability, and initiative. We often fail to take responsibility because we "lock in" our excuses and "lock out" why we are accountable. To make this point, here are some examples of excuses:

- Past experiences: not being selected for promotion
- Present circumstances: the recession and high unemployment
- People in our lives: parents, boss, spouse
- Personal weakness: procrastination, compulsive habit

We are touched and necessarily affected emotionally by these things. We are not and should not allow ourselves to be defined or determined by them. It is precisely because of these things that we must take responsibility and ownership of our thoughts, beliefs, emotions, attitudes, and actions. We are not prisoners of our past, nor do we need to be controlled by the events of our past. We are able to choose, and we are able to change. So our future is decided by how we choose to think about these things rather than by the impact of these things in and of themselves.

Note that each of the excuse bullets has the potential to become a significant "E" in our Events + Response = Outcome equation discussed in the introduction. Again, the key to success in our spiritual lives is how we choose to respond, and our response is framed in how we choose to see the event in the first place. When we fail to see significant life events and challenges with clarity, it is nearly impossible to respond to them with courage and trust in the will of God for all things, believing that God works all things to the good of those who love Him and are called according to His purpose (Rom. 8:28–29).

Note this wisdom from James Allen: "The outer world of circumstances shapes itself to the inner world of thought, and pleasant and unpleasant external conditions are factors which make for the ultimate good of the individual." Here again we discover a fundamental truth about owning our thoughts and taking responsibility for our outcomes. *Good thoughts and actions can never produce bad results; bad thoughts and actions can never produce good results.* We really do reap what we sow. Sow bad thoughts, and reap bad results. Sow good thoughts, and reap good results.

> Circumstance does not make the man; it reveals him to himself.
> —James Allen

Summary

Our habits are part of a cause-and-effect relationship between what we believe to be true about the world around us and the coinciding mental maps and patterns our brains create to align with those beliefs. It is amazing what happens in the lives of people when they dramatically change their thoughts (renew their minds) and experience the coinciding transformation of their circumstances and outcomes. Consider these contrasting patterns. Thoughts of fear and doubt create circumstances of failure and blame-shifting. Energizing thoughts create circumstances of hope and accomplishment. Hateful thoughts create circumstances of strife and conflict. Forgiving thoughts create circumstances of peace and reconciliation.

> You live with your thoughts so be careful what they are.
> —Eva Harrington

Sustaining personal change in order to drive high-performance behavior requires us to take responsibility and ownership of self by recognizing our habits, understanding how those habits impact and affect the people around us, and then taking consistent, deliberate, and disciplined actions to change and improve. Here are several key concepts to learn and apply daily as habits of your changing thinking and behavior.

Be accountable. Take responsibility for your decisions and actions. When you make a mistake, admit it, fix it, and learn from it. Have zero tolerance for excuses, and work to eliminate them from your daily behavior.

Let go of the past. If you are still reacting to a painful event in the past, let it go. The first step to a better future is to give up your hope for a better past. If you persist in a particular train of thought, whether good or bad, you will produce the results of those thoughts in your behavior and your circumstances.

Take ownership of your circumstances. Does it make any sense to willfully choose disruptive and unproductive behavior and circumstances in your life when you have a positive alternative? Even if your circumstances are unpleasant or uncomfortable, you do not have to be the cause of an event in order to be responsible for how you respond. You are responsible for how you respond to circumstances—even those you did not create.

Change yourself. Don't complain about a problem. Rather, take action and solve it. Our world is full of complainers and whiners. What we need are more problem solvers. Be a problem solver. Focus on what you can control, not on what you can't control. There are some things in life over which you have no control. Do not waste valuable time and energy on things you cannot influence. Focus on what you can control, beginning with yourself.

Develop the habit of asking proactive questions. Given the outcome I want and the event I am experiencing, what response on my part would be most effective? Am I clear about the goal I am pursuing? Do I see the situation clearly? What are my options for taking effective action? Don't be inactive or reactive. Be proactive.

Journal Exercises

Answer these questions:

I could dramatically improve the quality of my home life if I chose to:

I could dramatically improve the quality of my professional life if I chose to:

I could dramatically improve the quality of my relationship with my _____ if I chose to: (fill in the blank).

Here are some additional exercises:

1. The truth is that any problem you are currently experiencing, personally or professionally, can be directly linked to some repetitive bad habit. Do you agree or disagree with this statement? If you disagree, ask yourself why you disagree. Are you in denial about this bad habit, defending this bad habit, or simply dismissing this information as lacking any intellectual credibility? If you agree with this statement, are you willing to begin to learn how to change your bad habits?
2. Before any real change can take place in our lives, we must come to the point of being mentally convinced that change is real and possible and that it holds the promise of better, more enhanced, and improved outcomes. We must be ready to change.

    - What do you allow your mind to dwell on?
    - When things slow down and you have time for personal reflection, what thoughts come to your mind? The apostle Paul encouraged us to take every thought captive.
    - Do you find yourself constantly dwelling on negative things? If so, why?

- Can you begin to see and believe that in the daily practice of self-awareness you can actually control your thoughts and better manage your relationships with others?

3. Self-centeredness linked with a lack of self-discipline is a recipe that causes people to lose the quality of being teachable. Being teachable means you have the desire to learn from others. Self-pity is the enemy of growth and spiritual development.

- How open are you to learning from others?
- Would you consider yourself a person who is not open to learning from others? If so, what would it take for you to change and become more teachable?
- How would your family members answer this question about your willingness to learn from others? Are you willing to ask any of them? Can you see yourself becoming more willing to seek out advice and assistance from the knowledge and expertise of others if you knew it would improve the overall quality of your spiritual life?

Remember This

We must be very careful about the thoughts we allow in our minds. Our thoughts affect our emotions and our behavior. Consequently, we will always feel in accordance with the way we see and think. If you want to change your feelings, all you need to do is change your thoughts. Thinking is an active process that you should manage so that you see and think in ways that get you what you truly desire.

Now would be a good time to pray as well.

"Dear heavenly Father, I need Your help to change. I want to be in a rich, complete, loving relationship with You. I have been stuck so long in bad thinking and behavior, unwilling to apply the truth of Your Word to my life. I always believed that Your Word was true for other people but not for me. Forgive me. Renew a right spirit within me. Help me to believe that I can change with Your power, Your guidance, and Your direction for my life. Fulfill Your plan and purposes for my life as You desire. Make me an instrument of Your love and grace to others, that I may be a part of completing Your plan for the redemption of every lost person in the world. In Jesus's name I pray, amen."

PART III

Knowing Yourself and Managing Yourself Well with Others

"And behold, a certain lawyer stood up, and tempted him saying, 'Master, what shall I do to inherit eternal life?'" (Luke 10:25). This was a very important question if this expert in the law of Moses really wanted a definitive answer. Jesus did not answer the question but responded with a question of his own. Paraphrased, Jesus said, "You are a smart guy. You are an expert in the law. How do you answer your own question?"

The man answered, "You shall love the Lord your God with all your heart, and with all your soul, and with all your strength and with all your mind; and you should love your neighbor as you love yourself" (Luke 10:27). Jesus told him that he had answered correctly. Then Jesus told him to go do this in daily practice. The man knew what the law said in Deuteronomy and Leviticus, and Jesus told him, "Now go live it in your daily behavior."

Are you surprised that Jesus did not tell this man he had to be born-again? Are you surprised that Jesus did not offer him what he offered to the woman at the well in Samaria? According to the law of Moses, the man did answer correctly. *If* he could always love God, and *if* he could always love his neighbor as he loved himself, then he could have eternal life because he would be without sin. Jesus was trying to show him that no one can keep the law perfectly, so no one can have eternal life by his or her own merit or actions. Sadly, this man was not looking for the real answer but only justification for his own belief. His next response revealed his heart: "But he, seeking to *justify himself*, said unto Jesus, 'And who is my neighbor?'" (Luke 10:29, emphasis added).

As believers we too are to love God with everything we have within us. This ultimate desire to love God is supposed to fuel our obedience. We too are to love one another and put the needs of others above our own physical and material needs. The Bible says that this is how the world will know we are disciples of Jesus: by how we love one another. To live as abundant-life believers, we must not only know ourselves and manage ourselves well, but we must know ourselves and manage ourselves well *with others*. One is a requirement for a vertical relationship with God, and the other is a horizontal relationship with other people. Consequently, we will focus on how to manage ourselves well in relationship with God and our fellow human beings as a means of expressing the nature of Christ within us as we pursue a more abundant life.

Therefore, having a desire to change, and knowing *what* we need to change and *why* we should change, the process of undergoing real change is not just for our benefit as an end itself. Our change, its struggle, and the spiritual journey to conform to the nature of Jesus Christ is a means of effectively taking the gospel into the lives of other people. Failing to change into the image of Christ is arguably one of the most selfish acts any believer can commit. While too many people look weak and weary and claim to be victims of life circumstances as an excuse for not changing, at the root of the failure to change is pride. We simply love ourselves too much to change.

Note the statement of the lawyer again: "What must I do to inherit eternal life?" We need to examine three key words in this statement to see how self-love—expressed as both self-reliance and self-pity—is evident in this worldly attitude. Those words are *what*, *I*, and *do*.

1. *What* – Asking "what must I do" implied that there was something he could do to ensure that he would inherit eternal life. Jesus did what was necessary for us to have eternal life, in that while we were yet sinners, the Bible says, Jesus died for us.
2. *I* – Note that this expert in the law placed the emphasis of eternal life on himself. He was going to do something that he could take credit for regarding his eternal destiny. Could he simply believe in Jesus Christ, in the scandal of death by crucifixion, in a crucified Messiah? Not this guy. Pride such as this is not just a sin by itself; it also defines the nature of all sin. This man was putting his pride, his belief in self-reliance, in place of God's redemptive plan of salvation.
3. *Do* – Sadly, far too many believers get in a hurry to do something for God rather than focus on what they are to become in Jesus Christ. Many writers have adequately discussed the need to focus on what we are to *be* in Jesus before we try to *do* something for Jesus. We all could stand a good dose of repentance for our self-reliance and self-pity. Both reflect a great love of self, which we are to crucify daily (Gal. 2:20) so we can put on Christ in humility and acknowledge His love, grace, mercy, and tender peace. Do not be in a hurry to be doing things for God until you can adequately reflect His nature in you. Even the world has discovered that the greatest attribute of the most successful leaders in the world—the leaders others truly want to follow—is humility.

In this final section we will discover three key behaviors to managing ourselves well in our vertical relationship with the Father and our horizontal relationships with each other. These three behavioral skills include: managing emotion, creating and sustaining effective relationships, and communicating effectively to make positive connections with people so that we have access into their lives.

The means for developing these three skills remain Bible centered and cross focused. Neuroscience research has discovered facts about how God created us, and they play a part in forming the necessary habits to create and sustain highly effective relationships. They have a role to play in how we take responsibility for our thoughts, attitudes, emotions, and actions. They do not replace the preeminence of the Word of God as the source of all truth regarding our spiritual transformation. The answer to all of our spiritual struggles remains the truth of God's Word, faith, repentance, and God's grace. Then the peace of God, which passes all understanding, will dwell richly in your heart forever.

CHAPTER 7

Manage Your Emotions

> Your emotional memory provides a high gear that stimulates
> forceful self-regulated action for making new choices
> that move you toward what really matters in life.
> —Robert K. Cooper, neuroscience and leadership expert

Emotional Management

Emotional management is a personal performance competency. Achieving an abundant life in Jesus Christ requires that you learn how to manage emotion. No one else can manage your emotions for you. This is something you need to learn and apply consistently in the daily practice of abundant-life living. One thing is certain: if you do not manage your emotions and the energy these emotions create, then your emotions will manage you.

Emotions are a powerful force in our lives. We have all been in situations in which our emotions have energized us to perform with motivation, confidence, and a sense of purpose. We have all been in situations in which we have felt demotivated, discouraged, or angry and therefore have not chosen well and behaved ineffectively.

Emotional self-management was first defined in an article by psychologists Peter Salovey and John Mayer (1989–1990). Emotional self-management is simply the focused drive that all abundant-life believers need to achieve their spiritual goals. *It involves the ability to monitor one's own and others' feelings and emotions.* It includes achievement drive, initiative, optimism, adaptability, mental toughness, resilience, and emotional self-control. The capacity to strive to constantly improve and meet a biblical standard of spiritual excellence is *achievement drive*. *Initiative* is the readiness to act on opportunities, while *optimism* is persistence in pursuing goals despite obstacles and setbacks. *Adaptability* is the flexibility to handle change, and *emotional self-control* is the keeping of emotions and impulses in a balanced response to life events.

The Importance of Emotions

Our heavenly Father created our emotions. The expression of love in emotion is an expression of the nature of the Father. Can there be any more powerful statement of the emotion of love than John 3:16? This verse of the Bible is known and translated in more languages of the world than any other Bible passage: "For God so loved the world, that He gave His only begotten Son, that whosoever believes in him should not perish, but have everlasting life."

Here is what we know about emotions, both from the Bible and from neuroscience research.

"He that cannot rule over his own spirit is like a city that is broken down and without walls" (Prov. 25:28).

"But the fruit of the Spirit is love, joy, peace, longsuffering, gentleness, goodness, faith, meekness, temperance (self-control): against such there is no law" (Gal. 5:22–23).

"Therefore, my beloved brethren, let every man be swift to hear, slow to speak, slow to wrath: For the wrath of man does not work the righteousness of God" (James 1:19–20).

Pay particular attention to this next passage. It is foundational to this discussion on managing your emotions. Note that it starts out with a powerful positive emotion: rejoicing.

"Rejoice in the Lord always; and again I say, Rejoice! Be anxious for nothing; but in everything by prayer and supplication with thanksgiving let your requests be made known to God. And the peace of God, which passes all understanding, shall keep your hearts and minds through Christ Jesus. Finally brethren, whatever things are true, whatever things are honest, whatever things are just, whatever things are pure, whatever things are lovely, whatever things are of good report; if there be any virtue, and if there be any praise, *think on these things*" (Phil. 4:4–9, emphasis added).

How amazing it is that we receive from our heavenly Father—the creator of our emotions, not just in the mental sense of thought but also in the physical sense of a variety of neurochemicals—a prescription for managing damaged emotions, even new forms of therapy for post-traumatic stress disorder. As we can see from these Bible passages, God has something to say about emotions.

From the behavioral science work of Tim Kight, Robert Cooper, and a host of others, we can deduce the following:

- Emotions are a great amplifier. They intensify everything they touch.
- Emotions are not neutral. They are either your master or your servant.

- The emotions you feed will grow. If you focus on and feed negative or disruptive emotions, they will grow. If you focus on and feed positive and productive emotions, they too will grow.
- When you are caught in a negative emotional state, you empower the event (E) and decrease your ability to respond (R) effectively to people and circumstances (O).
- When you are in a positive emotional state, you empower your R and increase your ability to respond effectively to people and circumstances.
- Managing your emotions is a learned ability, not an inherited or instinctive one. Developing mental toughness is similar to developing physical strength and endurance. You must put stress on your emotions in order to improve your mental strength and endurance.
- Over time, neurochemicals like cortisol can damage your brain through a constant negative emotional state or a constant state of stress and anxiety, physically damaging the cells of the brain and altering the cell structure of chromosomes.
- Neurochemicals like endorphin, dopamine, oxytocin, and serotonin produce a positive physical effect on the brain, managing emotion, critical thinking capacity, positive relationship triggers, and overall superb mental health and enhanced immune capacity.

> Everything can be taken from a man but the last of human freedoms—the ability to choose one's attitude in a given set of circumstances, to choose one's way. —Viktor Frankl, *Man's Search for Meaning*

Self-management is an element of self-mastery. We have already discovered that these attributes are evident in daily and intentional practice in the lives of abundant-life believers. People who lack an understanding of self-management are ineffective in building highly effective relationships that support the development and progress of spiritual excellence. When people are unaware of how their disruptive emotions are affecting their own performance (self-awareness) they lack the ability to see how those emotions are affecting the performance (self-management) of the church.

It is clear from the Bible that God intended for us as believers to live in a common community. This community became known as the church. Sadly today, we can hardly claim to have come to an understanding of one baptism and one belief in Jesus Christ. Denominational differences have fractured the effectiveness of the gospel to change the world for good. Life might be great inside the denominations, but the world is falling apart around the church, and the church appears to be decaying from within as well—at least the church the Bible describes.

Read Ephesians 4:1–6 as a reminder and for the evidence for this claim: "I therefore, the prisoner of the Lord, beseech you that you walk worthy of the calling whereby you were called, with all lowliness and meekness, with longsuffering, forbearing one another in love; endeavoring to keep the unity of the Spirit in the bond of peace. There is one body, one Spirit, even as you are called in one hope of your calling: One Lord, one faith, one baptism, One God and Father of all, who is above all, and through all, and in you all."

It is imperative that we develop the attribute of emotional management in a cooperative effort among believers within the church. As Paul and other early church leaders developed mental toughness to manage the elements that trigger emotion and to manage emotions effectively in daily ministry, we too must acquire the resolve to mimic them in our own daily life events and interpersonal relationships.

One of the most powerful forces in your life is your acquired level of mental toughness. Mental toughness is the ability to stay motivated and focused on what you need to do, even in the midst of distractions, difficult circumstances, and disappointment. Achieving your spiritual goal of abundant life in Jesus Christ in today's emotionally demanding and increasingly stressful world requires high levels of emotional management and mental toughness.

Spiritual leaders in the church often fail to recognize the significant impact that experiencing and responding to significant life events exerts on the overall performance of the spiritual life of believers within the community called the church. For most people, the greatest amount of emotional disruption that spills over into the spiritual community of the church happens every day in the workplace.

Bond University professor of management Cynthia Fisher conducted a study called *Emotions at Work: What Do People Feel and How Should We Measure It?* According to Fisher's research, the most common negative emotions experienced in the workplace are:

- Frustration/irritation
- Worry/nervousness
- Anger/aggravation
- Dislike
- Disappointment/unhappiness

These negative emotions exist and are common outside of work as well. We all have to deal with negative emotions at various times and places. Learning how to cope with and manage these feelings productively is more important than ever before. Christians are not immune from this negative stress on their own emotions and the toxic impact this stress places on their marriages, their families, and other important interpersonal relationships. After all, negative emotions can spread, and no one wants to be around a person who adds negativity to a group. The cost to workplace productivity as a result of negative emotions exceeds billions of dollars. The cost in human terms in the disruptive elements to marriages and families is immeasurable.

The key to managing this emotional disruption is recognizing what triggers your negative emotions, and which types of feelings you face most often. When those emotions begin to appear, you immediately need to use the tools you will learn in this chapter to stay balanced and focused on the fruit of the Spirit that is within you. Put your mind on these things, says the apostle Paul in Philippians. The longer you wait to confront these emotions with the Word of God, the harder it will be to pull yourself away from negative thinking, which flows into negative emotions, which then results in negative and disruptive behavior.

Today everyone is talking, writing, and teaching about employee engagement. Employee engagement—not employee satisfaction—drives performance, and engagement is powered by the compelling force of positive emotion. When business leaders manage emotions positively, they bring out the best behavior in their followers. How employees *feel* about their organization and their work plays a significant role in how well they *perform* in the technical elements of their jobs. How employees *feel* about their organization determines their level of commitment, retention, and willingness to *act* as an ambassador to the community on behalf of the organization.

Consequently, individual leader behavior becomes the single most important predictor of organizational performance. This is why Christians should be the most productive employees of any organization. We have a means of managing all this negative stress in ways that unbelievers lack, namely the power of the Holy Spirit within us and the fellowship of believers who encourage and support us in the midst of the greatest of life challenges. The greatest overcomers of the greatest life challenges never succeeded alone. They rallied their own personal wills and skills to change, and they created a strong sense of community will and skill as well.

Community and Its Role in Your Change

Have you ever wondered why God invented "church?" Why does the Bible say that we are not to forsake the gathering of the brethren? Why are we supposed to worship God together? Wouldn't it be easier if we could just worship God individually? There seem to be so many imperfect people in church who bother me. Do I really need to expose myself to so much drama?

Here is one key point of fellowshipping together. When you, as an individual, seek to manage emotional impulse, you are still being affected by emotional energy and some element of control created by a difficult situation or some other person. The impact of events and other people on your emotional state can severely affect your spiritual growth and can create a disengaged and dissatisfied spiritual life.

Part of God's purpose in putting us together in relationships with Him and with each other is to expose our own imperfections and sin so we become aware of our need to change to become more like Him. Remember the sporting shoe commercial decades ago: "I want to be like Mike." You could know about Michael Jordan, but that did not mean you really had a relationship with him. Wearing his shoes was supposed to bring you closer to him and to becoming a basketball wizard like him. So it is with our relationship with God and each other. We are supposed to be like Jesus. We are supposed to be changing to represent more of Jesus to both our heavenly Father and to one another.

> Churches that have a high level of positive, emotional connection are going to have people that are more productive; they work harder; they're happier; they stay longer; they come to church to grow in their gifts and to serve others in the body of Christ. We were created by God to serve Him in relationship and to serve one another as well. When we are serving, our brains produce neurochemicals that reinforce an emotional balance of peace, safety, harmony, and tranquility. We get our best "therapy" when we stop thinking of getting for ourselves and think about giving to others. —Michael E. Frisina

Most pastors are so unaware of the power of emotions to drive spiritual growth that they consistently underestimate the legitimate emotional needs of people. Once their church begins to exhibit an emotional deficit, people begin to complain and disengage. When this occurs, they always shift to characteristics of satisfaction as a means of compensating for the emotional deficit that is impacting their spiritual growth, commitment, and engagement in acts of service.

Understanding the Power of Emotion

It is worth repeating that understanding the power and importance of emotions to propel high levels of spiritual performance is essential for the overall spiritual success of individuals and churches. Understanding the power of emotions is only one part of the equation. Developing yourself into an abundant-life believer, someone who is going to make a difference in the lives of other people, requires not only learning to be aware of the power of emotions but managing that power effectively to drive performance to its highest level possible.

> Anyone can become angry—that is easy. But to be angry with the right person, to the right degree, at the right time, for the right purpose, and in the right way—that is not easy. —Aristotle, Greek philosopher

So, should you do what your emotions tell you to do? The answer depends on the situation. The challenge is to respond effectively to situations and to avoid overreacting to your emotional impulses. An impulse to act is part of every emotion. The anger impulse is to strike out or speak out. The fear impulse is to fight, flee, or freeze. The happiness impulse is to celebrate, laugh, and rejoice. The depression and sadness impulse is to withdraw and detach.

A balanced response lies in your ability to manage an impulse by exerting the power of choice inherent in every rational human being. Between every stimulus (E) and your response (R) a gap exists that allows you to think about and choose your response. Will you make a choice for gratification or for effectiveness? Will you make a choice to love or to hate, to give or to take? Will you react on impulse with disruptive emotion and unproductive outcomes, or will you respond productively to more effective outcomes? The choice is always yours to make, and you own it.

Depending on the situation, any emotion can be either productive or disruptive. An emotion is productive if it strengthens you and helps you take effective action, and if it enables you to respond proactively to a situation. Productive emotions are a source of positive energy that empowers you to perform at upper levels of your potential. An emotion is disruptive if it hinders you from taking effective action, and if it produces an inactive or reactive response to a situation. Disruptive emotions are a source of negative energy that hinders you from performing at your best.

Disruptive emotions rob you of a state of mind that allows you to choose to live as an abundant-life believer. This is why some people can live in material abundance and spiritual poverty, and others can live in material poverty and spiritual abundance. It all depends on your focus frame and perspective, on concentrating your efforts not on what is happening but on how you respond to what is happening to you.

In response to someone's trying to harm your family, anger can be proactive and productive. But in response to the behavior of a fellow believer who is challenging your "grace quota," anger can be reactive and disruptive. The emotions you feed will grow. Spiritually mature believers and emotionally intelligent people feed productive emotions. They don't feed disruptive emotions.

Consequently, emotions are a powerful force in our behavior and our lives. Emotions are not neutral to events and stimuli that come to have great significance to our sense of meaning, value, and purpose. Spiritual excellence in a demanding and ever increasingly stressful world requires a high level of emotional management, mental toughness, and focus.

The Power of Focus

The R-Factor by Tim Kight demonstrates the power of focus (how we choose to look at the events and circumstances of our lives) as a sequence in a chain reaction that connects feeling, energy, and action. Borrowing from the E + R = O equation seen previously, the "R" is a combination of cause-and-effect relationships between thoughts and emotions. Emotions tell us how we feel about what we are thinking. Since we can have close to fifty thousand thoughts per day, it is more practical to manage emotions as a means of "taking every thought captive." The way the process works looks like this:

Focus (what you are thinking about) + Feelings (the emotions created by your thoughts) = Action

The critical path illustrated above is the mental chain of events at the heart of emotional management and mental toughness. Focus feeds emotion. Emotion creates energy. Energy influences action. The key to managing your emotions is learning to manage this mental chain of events.

Unique to each of us—and driving this chain reaction of responses—is what researchers call a social/behavioral style: driver, expressive, amiable, and analytical. Each of these behavioral styles reflects our own set of emotional needs, and each has its own response to the effect of stress and other factors that meet or fail to meet those emotional needs. As the pathway above illustrates, emotions do not respond directly to an event; rather, emotions respond to what you *think* about an event. Your thoughts and self-talk in response to an event create the emotions you have about the event. *To manage your emotions, you must manage your thoughts and control your mental focus.*

You write the scripts that you use to describe and interpret what you experience every day. You assign meaning to the events of life and work. What you focus on feeds your emotions. When you choose your focus, you choose your feelings. You are the author of the thoughts and self-talk that creates your feelings. If you want to change your feelings, change your focus.

Michael E. Frisina

The Emotional Element in Performance

Energy created by emotions strongly influences behavior. Consequently, abundant-life believers manage their spiritual life by continually managing their focus with great discipline. By "focus" I mean the sum total of their thoughts, inner self-talk, and scripted response to daily life events. The stuff of life is what happens in daily events. We are all aware of the key principle that it is not what happens to us that matters to the outcome but the way we *respond* to what happens to us that drives the outcomes of life events. What we see in these events is our perspective and our expectation of a positive or negative outcome, which will then create energy that compels us to act; it creates our behavior. Whether those feelings create, in the end, positive or negative outcomes depends on how a person chooses to focus on and respond to these daily life events, the daily living experiences we all share personally and professionally.

So our thoughts create emotions as a response to life events. This combination of thoughts and feelings produces four energy states:

1. High intensity of energy and positive feelings
2. Low intensity of energy and positive feelings
3. High intensity of energy and negative feelings
4. Low intensity of energy and negative feelings

We manage our emotional energy state by managing our mental focus. Emotions respond to how we think about an event or situation in our life. How you choose to remember previous life events and the emotions associated with those events feeds how you will respond or react to current and future events. For example, unresolved childhood trauma that manifests itself in negative stress, memories, and emotions can alter the structure of cells, affecting your immune system and contributing to multiple types of illnesses, which may occur ten to fifteen years after the original event. Physical illness robs people of abundant life and can have its origin in the lack of self-awareness and self-management of those early life events.

"Positive emotions help us live longer," says Donald Clifton. In their book, *How Full Is Your Bucket?*, Clifton and colleague Tom Rath show that positive emotions provide a buffer against negative health effects, anxiety, and depression. They enable us to recover faster from pain, trauma, and illness. They might even add more years to life expectancy than quitting smoking (5.5 years for men and 7 for women). Other studies suggest that positive emotions can even ward off the worst of the common cold.

Along with these physical benefits, positive emotions can produce benefits that add to our mental well-being, increasing our ability to function well in relationships and do well in all areas of life and work. Positive emotions, Rath and Clifton conclude:

- Protect us from and undo the effects of negative emotions;
- Fuel resilience and transform people;
- Broaden our thinking, encouraging us to discover new lines of thought or action;
- Break down racial barriers;
- Build durable physical, intellectual, social, and psychological resources that provide "reserves" during trying times;
- Produce optimal functioning in organizations and individuals; and
- Improve the overall performance of a group (when group leaders express more positive emotions).

Positive emotions generated by praise and accurate feedback increase peak performance in sports and learning and on the job. They improve marriages and relationships. They help us raise healthy, self-reliant, authentic, thinking children. Positive emotions are the driver for a life lived abundantly in Jesus Christ. If you are stuck in negative emotions, you cannot believe that Jesus died for you. If you are stuck in negative emotions, you will resist the truth that God loves you. If you are stuck in negative emotions and you resent the need of a Savior and the need to repent of your sins, then you will harbor resentment, bitterness, and unforgiveness toward others. If you are stuck in negative emotions, you will never fulfill the plan and purpose God has for your life.

Emotional Triggers

People who become behaviorally smart by learning to manage their emotions understand their own emotional triggers and the emotional triggers of people with whom they live in close relationships. Emotional triggers are people, events, conditions, or experiences that arouse intense negative reactions. Incompetence, micromanagement, constantly missing or incomplete information, an arrogant attitude, lack of communication, failed expectations, and excessive unproductivity in life events are just some of the emotional triggers existing in your daily life. Once triggered, an emotional reaction may stir up other negative memories and negate any positive experiences.

Close observation is the best way to learn about emotional triggers. Again, you own your response to life events. You must accept responsibility for learning about these triggers and discovering the impact they have on your emotional balance. Pay close attention to everything that is going on during an emotional interaction, including your own reaction. Immediately after the episode has passed, note your answers to the following questions in your journal:

- What triggered the event? (Write down a summary of what happened. Include background information, such as past discussions, responses, and compromises. Be detailed so that you can find cause-and-effect relationships among the specifics.)
- What emotions were felt and displayed? (It is easy to answer this question for yourself, but judge others' emotions by how they acted. Often body language is louder than actual words. This

is especially true of people who react passively. Make a list of your own and others' emotions, and then compare them. Are they similar or different, and why?)
- What words were exchanged? (These words are informative. In the heat of the moment, people are generally honest about their feelings and thoughts. If you listen carefully, you will find out a lot about what is working and what is not working.)
- How quickly did the situation escalate, and how long did it last? (This time sequence is important because it indicates how deeply the emotions were felt or how long they had been repressed. It could also signal how difficult or easy it will be to repair the relationship and correct the emotional trigger.)
- What are the emotional consequences of the event for you and for the others? (Make a list of the emotions you and others' displayed afterward—embarrassment, anger, sadness, relief, regret, and so on. Compare them. Are they similar or dissimilar, and why?)

Over time, observing these emotional reactions will provide insight into your emotional patterns. Then you can use this knowledge to better manage your emotions by changing your mental models, recalling supporting Bible passages, and praying for the Holy Spirit to help you keep in spiritual balance. By managing your own emotions, you are being mindful and considerate of others' emotions and avoiding their emotional triggers as well. In the fellowship of believers, you ultimately get to "be Jesus" and "do Jesus" to others, and they get to "be and do" Jesus to you.

Assessing Your Emotional Dimension

Assessment tools offer a powerful way to assess your strengths and weaknesses in emotional management. Just as you can take an assessment of your spiritual gift inventory, use the following tool to help you develop emotional awareness. Ask people in your inner circle of trust—in both your personal life and professional life—to complete the following assessment tool for you. Complete the assessment yourself and compare your responses to those who will complete it for you.

> Positive emotions are not trivial luxuries, but instead might be critical necessities for optimal functioning.
> —Barbara Fredrickson, positive psychologist

Emotional Awareness Questionnaire

Check off the best answer for each item. Answer the statements as honestly as possible. Ask yourself, "What do I really feel about this person?" If you are completing the questionnaire for someone else, do not write your name on this form.

Name of person being assessed, _____,

1. Is self-centered and disregards the feelings of others
   Yes____   No ____   Occasionally_____

2. Is a good listener and a wise teacher
   Yes____   No ____   Occasionally_____

3. Seeks out the counsel and opinions of family and friends before making important life decisions
   Yes____   No ____   Occasionally_____

4. Is calm and composed but responsive during a crisis or change effort
   Yes____   No ____   Occasionally_____

5. Talks with family and friends about the needs, goals, and problems of his or her life

Yes____   No____   Occasionally____

6. Complains about or procrastinates when dealing with difficult issues
   Yes____   No____   Occasionally____

7. Welcomes family and friends to provide feedback on his or her emotions and behavior
   Yes____   No____   Occasionally____

8. Is emotionally volatile, physically intimidating, and verbally abusive
   Yes____   No____   Occasionally____

9. Is involved in confrontation, conflict, and strife
   Yes____   No____   Occasionally____

10. Rewards and recognizes accomplishments
    Yes____   No____   Occasionally____

Please offer three suggestions to help this person improve his or her behavior.

1. _____
2. _____
3. _____

Summary

Behavior intelligence and managing emotions is personal spiritual competency. No one else can manage your emotions for you. This is something you need to learn and apply consistently in the daily practice of living an abundant life. One thing is certain: if you do not manage your emotions and the energy these emotions create, then your emotions will manage you. This is an essential element of spiritual warfare. Your adversary, the Devil, does not want you to live in emotional harmony. Satan does not want you to be victorious in this critical area of your life and spiritual development. Satan may not be able to rob you of eternal life, but he certainly desires to rob you of the plan and purpose God has for your temporal life.

Many extremely talented individuals, while highly effective in their talents and physical abilities, fail in their relationships with God and others because they lack behavioral, emotional, and interpersonal skills evident in the fruit of the Spirit. Behavioral skill development is essential for living an abundant life, in this world and in the coming kingdom.

Journal Exercises

Self-management requires that you pay attention to your internal conversations, those conversations you have with yourself. One of the greatest acts of personal responsibility you can take is to manage how your thinking, emotions, and behavior affect other people.

There is an old adage in organizational behavior that says, "People don't quit their jobs. They quit who they work for. They quit their leader."

1. What is your attitude toward the people you interact with daily? Do you treat people with respect, or do you use people as a means to an end? Do you routinely seek to manipulate people to get them to do what you need them to do? Do you see having to deal with "people issues" as a waste of your time?

You model for people your level of expectation for how they behave toward one another by how you behave toward them.

2. How often do you express your sincere appreciation to people and not merely "fake it to make it"? Do you believe sincere expressions of appreciation are legitimate and necessary to make positive, emotional connections with others? Would your family and close associates say you express sincere appreciation to them on a regular basis?

3. Do you feel appreciated by others? Do you often find yourself talking to yourself and saying, "Nobody loves me. Everybody hates me?" Remember this feeling because it is exactly how other people feel when you fail to express appreciation or you neglect to meet this legitimate emotional need for them.

4. Abundant-life believers have a keen awareness of their behavioral (emotional) skills. How accurately do you see yourself? Did you take the test in the middle of this chapter? How willing would you be to go to several people, tell them there is a specific change you want to make in your behavior, and ask them if they would let you know when you slip or lapse back into the old, ineffective behavior? As you seek to change your behavior, you will find that you are more aware of the change than other people are. Asking them to help creates a new impression and experience of yourself in your new behavior. The result will be a greater opportunity for influence with those people and a greater sense of emotional balance and well-being in your life.

Remember, abundant-life believers live in a constancy of purpose fueled by having settled the issue on the matter of how their behavior affects the lives of others and impacts their spiritual growth and development. How about you? Are you ready to change?

CHAPTER 8

Manage Your Communication

> Regardless of the size of your organization—whether it's a large corporation, a small company, a home-based business, or even your own family—you need effective communication skills if you want to succeed. The art of communication is the language of leadership.
> —James Humes

Do you know what activity you engage in the most as a human being? It is communication! Combine all the time you spend making and returning phone calls; sending and responding to e-mails and text messages; writing notes, memos, and reports; meeting with coworkers, customers, and vendors; making presentations; spending time with your family; and the like. You'll probably find that 70 to 90 percent of your total waking hours involve some form of communication.

Communication is essential to everything you do in life. You cannot be involved in highly effective relationships if you cannot communicate well. Effective communication begins or ends all forms of collaboration in our families, work environments, and effective ministry efforts. But we have multiple excuses for not improving our communication skills. Communication expert Bob Biesenbach states, "In over 25 years of professional life, I've heard every excuse there is for not making communication a priority in an organization. And I've heard them from every source: indifferent leaders, risk-averse lawyers, sluggish communication departments—you name it."

The biblical implications of communication are clear in James 3:2–13. In this passage, James began by telling us that the person who does not offend anyone with his words (communication) is perfect.

> For in many things we offend all. If any man offend not in word, the same person is a perfect man, and able also to bridle the whole body. But we put bits in the horses' mouths that they may obey us; and we turn about their whole body. Behold, also ships, which though they be so great, and are driven of fierce winds, yet are they turned about with a very small helm, wherever the helmsman turns it. Even so the tongue is a fire, a world of iniquity; so is the tongue among our members, that it defiles the whole body, and sets on fire the course of nature; and it is set on fire of hell. (James 3:2–6)

We all know that we have failed in communication—by inattention or accident, and certainly when we intend to do so. James went on to tell us that the tongue is a raging fire, full of deadly poison. Finally, he concluded that a wise man who is full of knowledge reveals himself with good conversation and meekness in wisdom. So we are without excuse in knowing how to communicate effectively. Or are we?

The Excuse Trap

Below are the most common excuses for disrupting effective communication or for sustaining ineffective communication. You have probably come across these in your own life, predominately at work. Maybe you have even used them yourself a time or two. Here is why they are a hindrance to performance and how you can overcome them.

1. *We can make it better.*

    Do documents and publications in your company routinely get caught in a perpetual churn cycle, where people offer endless edits that add little in the way of real value? That may be the sign of a dysfunctional organization. If people are fussing over every detail of a speech or web page for weeks or even months, how are they handling the really big decisions?

    These so-called perfectionists mistake changes for improvements and activity for action. So, tighten the review circle, identify the bottlenecks, and cut them out of the process. Enlist a high-level ally if necessary. Enforce quick deadlines, demand fast turnarounds on approvals, and use the old line: "If we do not hear from you by [x date/time], we will assume it's okay to go forward." Perfectionism is a vice, not a virtue. We can commit to excellence, and we should, but perfection is impossible, even for the perfectionist.

2. *We don't have all the information.*

    When do we ever enjoy the luxury of having *all* the necessary facts at hand? Even in an age where the information spigot is wide open and always gushing data, it's a rarity.

    So don't bother waiting. Come to terms with the fact that just about anything you communicate these days is out-of-date the instant you say it. Send it or post it. The best you can do is to tell people what you know, when you know it, and promise to get them the rest of the information as soon as you get it. Silence is not a good alternative. Gossip abhors a vacuum and will always fill a silent gap. When people in close relationships do not know why you are behaving the way you do, and when they are unwilling to communicate with you about it, they will make up a reason, and it will always be wrong.

3. *They'll ask a question we can't answer.*

   So? Get over the fear of being labeled uninformed or out-of-the-loop just because you can't answer a question. Nobody is expected to know everything, and those who try to do so create nothing but aggravation for themselves and those around them.

   Here's a simple answer for any situation in which you are unsure: "I don't know." Deliver it without apology or shame, and people will admire your self-confidence. What a delightful contrast to those who regularly demonstrate that they too don't know—but using twenty times the number of words. Of course, "I don't know" should be followed quickly by "but I'll find out and get back to you." Follow-up and reliability are essential to all highly effective relationships, whether with a spouse, children, boss, or coworkers.

4. *They've already been told.*

   Have they really? How and by whom? And if they have been told, do they understand? Don't assume. We all know that a message requires lots of impressions before it sticks, but many people need to be reminded of this fact.

   People often have a blind spot when it comes to their own communications. They can't bear the thought that people aren't hanging on their every word. So, one e-mail or presentation or web posting won't cut it. The message has to come through multiple channels and sources. Social media is an even worse place when it comes to people believing that everyone is involved with their personal lives. Are you worried about sounding repetitive, or people getting bored? Honestly, we should be so lucky to get that level of attention. It's important to overcommunicate because people tend to "under-listen" in this social media deluge of self-focus.

5. *We don't have time.*

   Lack of time, of course, is the mother of all excuses, and it's certainly not exclusive to communication. The fact is that we make time for the things that are important to us. If someone isn't taking the time to communicate, he doesn't consider it a priority. Or, as Lao Tzu, the ancient father of Taoism, put it: "Time is a created thing. To say 'I don't have time,' is like saying, 'I don't want to.'" Make the time to communicate. And don't let fears or false assumptions get in the way.

We Cannot Overcommunicate

Can we place too much emphasis on the need for open and effective communication? There are entire books, lectures, and even professional organizations dedicated to researching and improving overall communication effectiveness. Multiple studies show that ineffective communication is the root cause of dysfunctional personal and professional relationships. All of this attention on communication says to us: (1) it is critical to individual personal and professional harmony and (2) we all still struggle with open and effective communication.

Communication connects you to—or disconnects you from—customers, clients, coworkers, and prospects, as well as family and friends. The quality of your personal and professional relationships is profoundly affected by your ability to communicate effectively. The challenge in creating effective communication is to improve your behavioral competency to better understand the message you actually want to send, while adapting to the behavioral style of your intended receiver. This is most essential with people who tend to be unlike you in thinking, behavior, and communication styles.

Making the Connection

Communication is about connecting with people. Despite our best intentions, we do not always hear what is said, and we do not always say what we mean in a way that is easily understood. As a result, we do not always make the connection. Yet the apostle Paul wrote, "Let your speech always be with grace, seasoned with salt, that you may know how you ought to answer every man" (Col. 4:6). We are required to find a way to connect with people and to communicate effectively to maximize relationships and enhance ministry opportunities.

"What we've got here is a failure to communicate," says the captain in the Paul Newman classic film, *Cool Hand Luke*. This quotation articulates the communication challenges endemic in most of our lives today. The purpose of communication is to get your message across to others clearly and unambiguously. The greatest obstacle to communication is the illusion that it has taken place. We think what we say is clearly understood by others, only to find out later that others really do not have a clue what we intended.

Communication is very challenging because there are so many moving parts and so many opportunities for misinterpretation. Avoiding these problems requires effort from both the sender of the message and the receiver. And it's a process that can be fraught with error, with messages often being misinterpreted by the recipient. When this isn't detected, it can cause tremendous confusion, wasted effort, and missed opportunity.

In fact, communication is only successful when both the sender and the receiver understand the same information as a result of the communication. By successfully getting your message across, you convey your thoughts and ideas effectively. When not successful, the thoughts and ideas that you convey do not necessarily reflect your own, causing a communications breakdown and creating roadblocks that stand in the way of your goals, both personally and professionally. Disrupting communication among believers is a key strategy of our spiritual enemy. Whether impeding the arrival of a spiritual message from an angel to a prophet, or creating a division among the original apostles regarding ministry vision, communication breakdowns take a toll on spiritual development and spiritual effectiveness in ministry.

Communication barriers can pop up at every stage of the communication process, which consists of source (sender), encoding (message), channel, decoding, receiver, feedback, and context. These barriers have the potential to create misunderstanding and confusion. To be an effective communicator, and to get your point across without misunderstanding and confusion, your goal should be to lessen the frequency of these barriers at each stage of this process with clear, concise, accurate, well-planned communications.

Finally, you must be committed to self-control. The apostle Paul encouraged us, "Let no foul or corrupt communication come out of your mouth, but that which is good for the purpose of edifying [building up and encouraging] that it may minister grace unto the hearer." Did you ever consider that your words were meant to be an instrument of God's grace? How do you reconcile that biblical requirement with the negativity that can flow so easily from your heart?

Four Steps to Effective Communication

While the biblical mandate is clear, your practical ability to communicate and connect with others, to build them up and encourage them, is determined by how effectively you do four things. Communication experts all seem to agree on these key elements of effective communication listed below:

1. Care deeply
2. Listen carefully
3. Communicate your message effectively
4. Adjust your behavior style appropriately

If you are a ministry leader or a parent communicating with your children, consider this. The four steps of communication are essential for connecting with people and teams. People respond to leaders who care, listen, and communicate a clear and consistent message. People respond to leaders who are flexible in adjusting their behavior style. People resist leaders who don't seem to care, don't listen, don't communicate clearly, and have an inflexible style.

If you are on a ministry team or in a family, effective teams have people who collaborate by caring, listening, communicating, and flexing their behavioral styles to work together to achieve a common goal.

If you are married, a healthy marriage is built on a foundation of caring, listening, communicating, and adjusting.

If you have children, the four elements are essential for connecting with kids. Children need and want parents who care, listen, communicate, and are flexible in adjusting their style.

The Four Steps in Action

1. Care deeply.

Caring is the ultimate connector because it creates an emotional connection with people. People don't care how much you know until they know how much you care. People remember you not because of what you say but because of how you make them feel. Remember that caring is not always a feeling; sometimes it is a choice. Caring is a value-based decision, not an emotion-based decision.

Here is the key to caring: find out what is important to the other person, and make it important to you in a way that they can feel it. The first task is to be interested, not interesting. Ask yourself, "What is important to this person? What does the situation feel like from this person's perspective?" Each behavioral style has its own particular level of empathy associated with it. (Refer to appendix 1). People with styles 1 and 4 will have to pay closer attention to balancing their focus between an emphasis on tasks and an emphasis on paying attention to people.

2. Listen carefully.

Listening is about discovery. It is one of the most important ways of connecting with others. If you don't listen, you cannot communicate effectively. Listening is essential to making a positive connection with people. People do not always want or need to be agreed with; they do want to be heard and understood. Understanding occurs at the intellectual level (a person believes you understand what they are saying) and at the emotional level (a person believes you understand what they are feeling). People with behavioral style 2 must focus on listening more carefully, as they tend to talk more and listen less.

Caring guides the way you listen. When you lack a caring attitude, you don't listen for all the facts and feelings. You listen selectively. You listen for what you want to hear. You listen for things that defend your position and weaken the other person's position. You listen from your own perspective, not the other person's perspective. When you lack a caring attitude, your focus is on yourself, not on the person with whom you are trying to connect.

Listening is a mental discipline. Listening challenges are often caused by decreased attention levels (another tendency for people with behavioral style 2) and increased stress levels. When you are distracted or not fully tuned in to another person and his message, you are apt to miss the intended meaning. The mind processes information at about 400 to 600 words per minute, but the average speaker sends 125 to 150 words per minute. The differences in speed often cause our minds to drift away from listening. To improve your listening, use the FOCUS technique below.

- *Focus* on the person. Set aside your agenda and your ego. Try to understand his perspective and particular situation. Find

out what is important to that person and make it important to you.
- *Observe* verbal and nonverbal signals. Note the person's facial expression, body language, and tone of voice. Pay attention to what the person is saying.
- *Clarify* and verify to make sure that what you are hearing is what the other person is saying. Ask great questions. Stop occasionally and summarize.
- *Use* body language that says "I am listening and I care." Maintain appropriate eye contact. Don't fiddle with your hands or with pens or pencils. Vary your body posture during the discussion: sit up to signal alertness, lean forward to signal interest, and sit back to signal reflection and a relaxed attitude.
- *Seek* to understand facts, feelings, and assumptions.

3. Communicate your message effectively.

When you send a message, whether by speaking, writing, or other methods, you are trying to convey a particular meaning. You want the listener to hear, understand, and respond to your message and its meaning. You want to connect. Here are some tools, tips, and techniques for communicating your message effectively.

- Be prepared. Know what you want to say. Organize your thoughts and ideas.
- Be clear, concise, and compelling.
- Think before you speak. Smart people know what to say. Wise people know *whether* to say it and when to say it if they do. This includes electronic forms of communication, including e-mails and text messages.
- Manage your behavioral responses. Mismanaged behavior creates distorted messages. Manage your emotional process through *focus, feelings, energy,* and *action*. Choose not to

communicate when you are in a high or low negative emotional state. (Refer to chapter seven on how to manage emotions.)
- Pay attention to how you communicate verbally, vocally, and visually:
  - *Verbally* - use words that communicate, illustrate, and motivate. What messages are you are sending with your words? Mark Twain said that the difference between the right word and the almost-right word is the same as the difference between "lightning" and "lightning bug."
  - *Vocally* - manage the inflection, tone, and volume of your voice. What message are you sending with your tone of voice?
  - *Visually* - engage with eye contact, body language, and facial expression. What message are you sending with your body language and facial expression?
- Eliminate audible pauses and verbal fillers such as "ah," "um," "you know," and "like." Be comfortable with silence. Learn the power of the pause.
- Listen as you communicate. Observe nonverbal responses.
- Check for understanding. Ask confirmation questions.
- Practice, practice, practice! Make an audio recording of yourself and listen to the playback. Record a video of yourself and watch the playback. There is no better way to get feedback about your communication strengths and weaknesses than to watch and listen to yourself deliver a message.

4. Adjust your behavioral style.

Effective communication requires that you learn to adjust and adapt the communication strengths and weaknesses of your behavioral style. Key communication disconnects are frequently related to behavioral style. Each behavioral style has its own unique way of communicating and connecting. You tend to communicate and connect with people who are more like you in your thinking, communicating, and behavioral style. The key is in being effective with people who are *not* like you.

Your level of self-awareness in knowing your own style and the styles of others, and in flexing these styles in all the various modes of communication is essential to clear and concise understanding, execution, and performance. Remember this: your behavioral style affects all four elements of communication: the way you care and listen, the way you convey your message, and the way you flex and adapt to the styles of other people.

Summary

Communication, at a minimum, requires the exchange of thoughts, information, ideas, and opinions. Communication is a necessary and essential element of collaboration and connection. It is a key characteristic of high-performing organizations. It is impossible to drive and sustain performance without consistent, effective communication. It is equally difficult to create and sustain highly functional relationships without the same commitment to consistent, effective communication. Improving communication begins with improving our behavior. The challenge is clear. Without immediate and consistent improvement in communication, efforts to create collaborative cultures of performance excellence will continue to fail.

Journal Exercises

Do you believe you currently possess the behavioral skills essential to creating and working and living in harmony with others?

- Do you have a tendency to seek out opportunities to work within a group? If not, why not?

- Are you comfortable with shared decision making, or do you prefer to make independent decisions?
- Are you aware of your behavioral/social style and its impact on your willingness and preferences in cooperating with others or "going it alone?"
- What advantages can you see for developing your spiritual influence if you adopt a more collaborative approach with others?

Are you prepared to work in relationships with other people? Stanley Allen wrote, "The most useful person in the world today is the man or woman who knows how to get along with other people." Not everyone has developed the skill to create and sustain healthy relationships.

- Are you a person regarded by others as someone who knows how to get along with other people?
- Do you find yourself in the midst of conflict and strife as a regular daily occurrence? If so, why?
- Are you a person who struggles with interpersonal relationships?
- Are you ready to learn and apply fundamental principles to overcome relational blind spots that are impacting your spiritual growth and development? What would it take for you to be more open in developing effective relationships?

John Maxwell said, "Our ability to build and maintain healthy relationships is the single most important factor in how we get along in every area of life."

- What are your greatest moments of success and failure? Did you ever consider that your moments of success were dependent on relationship? Did you ever consider that your failures were too?
- Have you ever considered how the effectiveness of those relationships is impacting your ability to achieve your personal goals? Have you ever given anyone permission to provide you

with feedback on the effectiveness of your relationships? If yes, what did that person tell you?
- Did you change anything about your behavior as a result of the feedback?
- The growth and development of people is arguably the greatest responsibility of spiritual leadership. Are your people following you as their spiritual leader? When you have an idea, how hard is it for you to get your idea across to others and get them on board with supporting change?
- Do you find yourself isolated from others and having to "go it alone" to get things done and make things happen? If so, why do you think that is the case?
- What could you change about yourself to create more cooperative and collaborative relationships with other people?

Effective communication skills require a high level of self-awareness. To be an effective spiritual leader or simply to live an abundant life, understanding your personal behavioral style of communicating is a requirement for spiritual growth. If you invest in this area of major change in your life, you will go a long way toward creating positive and lasting impressions with others. By becoming an effective communicator, you will improve your productivity as well as your ability to influence, persuade, and negotiate. What's more, you'll avoid conflict and misunderstandings. All of these are necessary for spiritual effectiveness and success in making a difference in the lives of other people.

CHAPTER 9

Manage Your Relationships

> Unity is strength ... When there is teamwork and collaboration, wonderful things can be achieved.
> —Mattie Stepanek, poet

Jesus Loves Me

The model we have for our horizontal relationships with other people stems from the practice of our vertical relationship with our heavenly Father. When teaching His disciples how to pray in Luke 11:2–4, Jesus started with the phrase "Our Father." This is a radical shift from the way Jewish people would have begun prayer. The use of the word *father* would have been too familiar, too casual, too disrespectful, and too irreverent. It just would not have been religiously dignified in their culture.

That should not be the case with us. When we pray, when we talk to God, we need to see Him as a loving heavenly Father. One way I maintain this perspective is through the wonderful song "Jesus Loves Me." During my military assignment at West Point, my wife was curator of the Constitution Island museum. How wonderful it was to know that the island was the home of Anna Bartlett Warner and her older sister Susan. Anna wrote the words of the song as a poem, and they first appeared in a book written by Susan. The words were set to a tune by William Bradbury in 1862, and a copy sits on the organ in the parlor of the Warner house. Originally published in 1860, it appeared in three stanzas:

Jesus loves me—this I know,
For the Bible tells me so;
Little ones to him belong.
They are weak, but he is strong.

Jesus loves me—loves me still,
Though I'm very weak and ill;
From his shining throne on high,
Comes to watch me where I lie.

Jesus loves me—he will stay,
Close beside me all the way.
Then his little child will take,
Up to heaven for his dear sake.
(Susan Warner and Anna Bartlett Warner, *Say and Seal* [Lippincott & Company, 1860], 115–116)

The words of this song are a constant reminder that my faith in God is based on personal relationship. Investing in this relationship makes the difference for me every day—when things are going well and in times of trial and testing—because "Jesus loves me. He will stay close beside me all the way." When you live your life on earth in a personal relationship with the Father, the Son, and the Holy Spirit, life gets exciting, interesting, and abundant, for you are living the perfect plan and purpose God, the Father, has for you. This joy of life is not meant to be lived alone. We were made to be in relationships and to collaborate with one another in fulfilling a collective purpose within the body of Christ, the church.

Michael E. Frisina

Effective Relationships: The Performance Difference

Collaboration enriches the lives of all people. It emphasizes the fact that all of us—no matter our position, power, status, or economic level—have something to contribute to the gospel and the kingdom of God. Our heavenly Father intends for all of us to live with meaning, worth, and value in our transformation to abundant-life believers. After all, when someone asks you to get involved or to help, you feel needed, valued, and desired as an integral part of something bigger than you alone. People who feel this way find their work meaningful, and as a result they willingly contribute their time, talent, and energy and are motivated to perform at high levels. At the least, these people become advocates or supporters of kingdom work. In this way, collaboration in highly effective relationships encourages people to work together to fulfill a mutual, beneficial, meaningful purpose in Christian fellowship.

The Bible Requires Us to Be in Effective Relationships

Once again we return to the apostle John and his emphasis through the Holy Spirit on our loving one another in Christian fellowship. "A new commandment I give unto you, that you love one another; as I have loved you, that you love one another" (John 13:34). When we fail to create highly effective relationships, it is impossible to create collaborations. The challenge for spiritual leaders is to observe, identify, and amend behavioral weaknesses so they can form highly effective relationships that, in turn, drive successful ministry collaborations.

Collaborations can be formed by any individual or group, but they cannot be sustained long enough to yield the desired results in the absence of highly effective relationships guided by a self-aware abundant-life believer. We do not work in isolation. God did not create us to be alone. Nearly everything we do requires that we connect and collaborate with other people.

The underlying message of this behavioral skill is that a culture of collaboration trumps competition in the quest to achieve performance excellence. But collaboration is not possible among people who do not cultivate the desire to be obedient to the Word of God. If you want to improve spiritual growth, you must begin paying attention to relationship dynamics. Becoming one with each other in a mutual, beneficial, meaningful purpose is the key to highly effective relationships. "And glory which you gave to me, I have given to them; that they may be one, even as we are one" (John 17:22).

Barriers to Transforming Your Relationship Mind-Set

Transforming an attitude from independent and competitive to interdependent and collaborative is not uncomplicated. Following are just some of the barriers to this transformational change.

- *Behavioral weaknesses* - According to research, high-performing professionals tend to share some performance strengths and weaknesses. The strengths include working memory, organizational ability, and planning/prioritizing. The weaknesses include stress tolerance, emotional control, and sustained attention (*Chief Learning Officer*, 2009). Note that the strengths are technical in nature, while the weaknesses are behavioral. The findings of this study support the argument made earlier in the chapter that, most of the time, behavioral weakness, not technical deficiency, is the main reason for a lack of collaboration, increased negative conflict, or failure in relationships. A person who continues to hone technical strengths but ignores the effects of behavioral weaknesses cannot expect (or will find it difficult) to create, let alone sustain, highly effective relationships.
- *Slow adoption of change* - We all tend to resist change, even change we want and desire. The problem in exporting ideas or

a mind-set of collaboration to current relationships lies in the slow process and people's resistance to change. Even when we are provided with facts and logical reasons to change, we are slow adopters of any change initiative.

- *Top-down decision-making structure* - Within an organization like a church, organizational performance is a leader's responsibility. Unfortunately, many leaders tend to take this duty literally, acting as the first and final decision makers on all financial and operational matters. So-called "solutions" are developed independently, creating more problems because these leaders lack the perspectives of the people who are directly affected by the implementation of these solutions. Many process improvements and change initiatives fail for this very reason. This top-down environment breeds cynicism, dissatisfaction, infighting, and other negative emotions and behaviors that are disruptive to highly effective relationships.

Key Relationship Killers

If you have ever occupied a leadership position, you have experienced some or all of the barriers to cultural transformation that would enhance relationships, teamwork, and collaboration. Creating a culture of collaboration means you must eliminate or mitigate behavioral weaknesses that disrupt communication, foster uncooperative attitudes, erode trust, and breed dysfunctional teams. Perhaps the most important part of this cultural change process is the influential leader's ability to guide others to conform to the desired mind-set and behaviors that create and sustain highly effective relationships. To do so, leaders must begin to eliminate the following relationship killers from the organizational culture and their internal relationships:

- Lack of integrity
- Self-centeredness

- Ineffective communication
- Misaligned or lack of clear expectations
- Emotional blackmail
- Unresolved conflict
- Gossip
- Taking more than one gives
- Negative attitude
- Not investing enough time and energy
- Failure to change and grow
- Failure to forgive/holding a grudge

Action Steps for Building Effective Relationships

> "Organizations typically spend considerable energy and effort in team building initiatives, including workshops, retreats, and adventure type experiences. While all of these have their place, if organizations want to increase collaboration and enhance teamwork, they need to start with trust."
> —Bruna Martinuzzi, emotional intelligence expert

Step 1: Build Trust

Trust is a complex and far-reaching concept that pervades our personal and professional pursuits. We cannot bottle and sell it, and we cannot fully appreciate its enormous role in shaping the constructs of society, including commerce, politics, and religion. Nonetheless, cultivating trust is an imperative, especially in organizational life. It increases the likelihood that people will engage and collaborate, communicate openly, adopt cooperative attitudes, and work in an integrated team with a shared responsibility for shared objectives. When trust is absent, damaged, or lost in the workplace, families, and churches, then relationships are dysfunctional, and effectiveness and performance suffer.

The word *trust* is derived from *trost*, a German term that suggests comfort. This is an appropriate association because when we trust someone we are comforted by the belief that this person has our best interest at heart and will not do anything to endanger us or put us at risk. Because trust is a critical component in all human interactions, it has many types. Following are two that are encountered the most in a team setting:

- Generalized trust – We trust on the basis of our mental model that people are generally trustworthy. It is a leap of faith, in that we choose to trust without evidence that our trust is deserved or without concrete assurance that the one we trust will deliver good results. As social and ethical theorist Russell Hardin (2002) puts it, "Generalized trust must be a matter of relatively positive expectations of the trustworthiness, cooperativeness, and helpfulness of others."
- Behavioral trust – We bestow our trust on the basis of a person's good behavior. That is, if someone has exhibited reliability, honesty, competency, compassion, or courage over time, that person earns our trust. *Earn* is the operative word here. Trust does not come automatically with positions of power. However, even if it did (as in the case with generalized trust), trust cannot be sustained by virtue of rank alone. It must be supported by ongoing good behavior, which then validates our confidence.

Trust-earning behaviors include the following:

- Consistency in manner, words, and actions
- Accountability and transparency, including active listening, sharing information, and taking responsibility instead of blaming
- Genuine or sincere interest in and concern for others
- Respectful and equal regard and treatment of others, regardless of rank or position

- Focused attention
- Principled and evidence-based decision making
- Dedication to fulfilling (not just making) promises
- Willingness to celebrate and reward good and exceptional work

These behaviors depict the self-aware traits of abundant-life believers. As masters of interpersonal relationships, they know that their everyday words and actions can either strengthen or weaken trust. People can only take so much bad behavior before they lose their faith and start to feel disconnected from other people and those relationships.

Awareness of your behavioral style is particularly important for creating trust and limiting negative, unproductive conflict. Understanding one another's behavioral style helps us develop trust in relationships and learn to communicate in healthy and productive ways. This provides a solid basis for managing the other key characteristics of highly functional relationships: commitment, accountability, and productive—or abundant—life outcomes.

In his book, *The Five Dysfunctions of a Team*, Patrick Lencioni states that trust lies at the heart of functioning, cohesive relationships, and that without trust those types of relationships and productive teamwork are all but impossible. Members of trusting teams admit weaknesses, take risks by offering one another feedback and assistance, focus their energy on important issues, and are willing to ask for help. Teams that use a focused approach can achieve trust, and one of the best ways to do this is to manage your behavioral style profile purposefully and intentionally. The same is true within the biblical context of relationships within the church.

Your behavioral style profile focuses on key aspects of your behavior, the things you typically say and do to other people. (Refer again to appendix 1. It provides a very clear description of people's strengths and weaknesses, as well as insight into people's work preferences.) This knowledge is invaluable for creating an atmosphere of trust. People with differing behavioral styles often have a hard time working together, and this can lead to a breakdown of trust. This is particularly true for people who have opposite styles because their behavioral preferences are dramatically different from one another's. For example, during team meetings, an *expressive* person speaks loudly and frequently and likes to make decisions quickly. In contrast, an *analytical* person speaks softly, less frequently, and wants to take time before coming to decisions.

Since these people's styles are at odds, their behavioral differences can lead to conflict and a lack of trust. By recognizing behavioral style differences, you will develop a better understanding and acceptance of one another. You will identify one another's strengths and weaknesses and will learn how to accept and capitalize on them. Since these differences are merely behavioral and are not a reflection of personal judgments or personality disputes, you will more easily develop a cohesive and trusting team that focuses on work rather than style differences.

Step 2: Make Communication a Priority

The purpose of communication is to get your message across to others clearly and unambiguously. Doing this involves effort from both the sender of the message and the receiver. It's a process that can be fraught with error, with messages often misinterpreted by the recipient. When this ambiguity isn't detected, it can cause tremendous confusion, wasted effort, and missed opportunity.

In fact, communication is only successful when both the sender and the receiver understand the same information as a result of the communication. By successfully getting your message across, you convey your thoughts and ideas effectively. When you're not successful, the thoughts and ideas you convey do not necessarily reflect your own, causing a communications breakdown and creating roadblocks that stand in the way of your goals, both personal and professional.

In a recent survey of recruiters from companies with more than fifty thousand employees, communication skills were cited as the single most important deciding factor in choosing managers. The survey, conducted by the University of Pittsburgh's Katz Business School, points out that communication skills—including written and oral presentations and the ability to work with others—are the main factors contributing to job success.

In spite of the increasing importance placed on communication skills, many individuals continue to struggle with this. They are unable to communicate their thoughts and ideas effectively, whether in oral or written format. This inability makes it nearly impossible for them to compete effectively in the workplace, gets in the way of career progression, and plays havoc in creating and sustaining highly effective personal and professional relationships.

When people in relationships have a trust foundation, they communicate openly and honestly. They first care deeply about one another, listen carefully to each other, and clearly communicate ideas and issues with each other. When we choose not to communicate effectively, openly, and honestly in relationships or teams, our conversations typically turn to gossip and manipulative, self-oriented exchanges of words. With the advent of social media, the issue of effective communication is compounded by texting and e-mail. Nothing can take the place of a face-to-face conversation between two people for effective communication.

To make communication a priority, we can use this proactive question: given the outcome I want and the events I am experiencing, what communication response on my part would be most effective? When we are proactive in our communication rather than inactive or reactive, we are thoughtful, disciplined, and fully engaged in making positive, productive connections with other people.

Failure to be proactive in communication contributes to a number of causes that lead to ineffective performance in both organizational and human factors. It is well documented that time pressures, work stress, a multilayered corporate structure, language incompatibilities, and information overload are some of these organization-related causes.

The human factors are mental, behavioral, and emotional weaknesses, such as the following:

- Poor listening skills
- Lack of focus, or mental disorganization
- Impatience and arrogance
- Tendency to assume instead of double-check
- Uncontrolled emotional attachment or response to the information
- Disinterest in the information or the task
- Refusal to clarify and follow up
- Fatigue or burnout

People who display these and similar interpersonal inadequacies put themselves, their communication partners, and those affected by the information in a dangerous position. They send and receive only partial—and possibly incorrect—information, and consequently they create time-consuming doubled work, confusion, frustration, and conflict. In this case, communication will not improve if behaviors and mind-sets do not improve.

Impact of Behavioral Style on Communication

Communication starts and stops all collaborations. We cannot begin to collaborate if we do not sit down for a discussion first, and we cannot continue our collaboration if we do not regularly communicate with our partners. Thus, effective communication is a critical trait, especially for a team or family composed of people with diverse behavioral styles.

Our behavioral styles (not to be confused with personality) are the way we present ourselves to those around us. We show our style by the way we interact with others, communicate, manage ourselves, receive and process information, and respond to situations. We can be *analytical*, a *driver*, *amiable*, or *expressive*. (Review appendix 1 for the definitions of and variations on these terms.)

Differing behavioral styles are necessary (and likely inevitable) in collaboration because we face so many issues that demand multiple, varied approaches. The challenge for all collaboration efforts is to learn each member's behavioral style so that all communications take advantage of the strengths of each style to yield productive or desired results.

The following suggests approaches you can take to improve your communication in relationships, teams, and collaborative partnerships.

These approaches work for both verbal and nonverbal exchanges with your personal and professional relationships.

1. *Don't condescend.* Condescension is a nuanced practice. Sometimes it's hard to tell if we or others are involved in a condescending exchange. Generally a statement that makes you sound superior to others and makes others feel inferior to you (and vice versa) is condescending. For example, "Let me put it in words you can understand" is condescending, and so is "I will repeat the information as many times as you need." Terms of endearment, e.g., "dear," "buddy," "sweetheart," "kid," no matter the intent, should also not be used in a professional setting. The key here is to regard your collaboration partners as equals, people who have as much to offer as you do, regardless of titles and ranks.
2. *Don't speak before you listen.* No one seems to be patient anymore in our twenty-four–seven world of information where news, data, opinions, and recommendations are within reach on the Internet and other electronic media. This constant accessibility has made us anxious to get to the "good part." As a result, when we interact with others we interrupt, we hear instead of listen, we get defensive, and we think of a quick response instead of focusing on what is being said. Listen with all your senses; this means paying attention to words, body language, tone, surroundings, and intent. Be aware of your own signals as well. Wait to speak;

view the process of conversation as a capital investment. You would not sign off on the purchase of an expensive piece of equipment in the middle of a cost analysis, so why would you respond before the other person can fully express the message?

3. *Don't be vague.* Be clear about your goals and expectations, and encourage others to articulate their wants and needs. This simple practice prevents you and your team from making assumptions, doing extra work, and accomplishing the wrong tasks or meeting the wrong targets. Follow up, clarify, repeat yourself, or write an outline, as necessary. The point of being clear is twofold: (1) to give collaboration partners a chance to disagree, ask questions, and offer compromises and (2) to ensure that all collaboration partners are headed down the same path.

4. *Don't withhold relevant information.* Provide needed resources to your team, including information that would enable the team to do its job fully and well. Insight, lessons, and advice from experience are as much information as facts and data. Share background, forecasts, current trends, and research findings, as well as negative and positive intelligence. Urge every team member to do the same, and help each other cultivate and maintain a trust culture in which the information shared will not be used for sabotage or damage.

5. *Don't ignore conflict.* Even the most benign interactions can cause conflict. Consider this brief instruction: "Please hand in your report next week." The lack of specifics in this note can infuriate a busy team member, making her feel defensive, for starters. Despite our general aversion to conflict, we have to face it. Pretending it does not exist will only enlarge it and ruin the good will we have built into our relationships with our collaboration partners. Listening, being objective, admitting to our mistakes and role in the problem, learning others' behavioral styles, keeping the situation fact-based instead of emotion-driven, and offering practical solutions are some ways to resolve and manage conflict.

Highly Effective Relationships and the Integrated Team

As stated earlier, anyone can put together an integrated team. But only an influential leader can create and sustain a highly functional integrated team. Sustaining such a team requires the leader to provide guidance and needed resources and then stay out of the way. Influential leaders know that micromanagement has no place in this equation. This is why they form teams whose members have behavioral competencies. These interpersonal skills enhance the team members' financial, operational, and human resource knowledge and abilities. If members cannot get through to other people, their technical expertise will not do much to advance the goals of the team. It is worth repeating: *technical skills rise no higher than individual behavioral skills.*

In virtually every organization, there is one person whom everyone regards as detrimental to the mission, vision, values, and strategies of the enterprise. This is a person who comes to work intent on making the lives of everyone else a nightmare. This is a person whom others would like to fire if they had the authority to do so. No organization—churches included—needs a team member like this. The organization cannot become what its people are not; that is, if employees are mediocre, the organization is equally mediocre. If a church member is toxic in behavior, the church will have a toxic behavior as well. None of this benefits the effort to create and sustain highly effective relationships and peak performance in fulfilling the purpose of the organization.

Ultimately, creating *and* sustaining a highly functional, integrated team requires developing strong interpersonal relationships. Remember that we never get the relationships we wish for, but we do get the relationships we work for. And working for effective relationships and teams involves doing the following:

- Asking more than telling
- Expressing thanks and appreciation in both formal and informal ways

- Including the group in brainstorming and problem-solving processes
- Being approachable
- Rewarding cooperative and interdependent behavior, not "rock star" performance
- Hiring people who value and understand shared responsibility and accountability
- Staying committed to collaboration, not competition and conflict

Journal Exercises

The following questions are intended to initiate self-examination of the trust that exists within your team and organization. Take the time to think about the questions posed here, and be honest with your responses.

- Do you share information (positive or negative) that is helpful to others, or do you withhold it?
- Do you treat everyone with kindness, respect, and compassion?
- Do you follow through on your commitments, even if it is at considerable personal expense?
- Why do you consider yourself a trustworthy person?
- What emotional reactions does your behavior bring out of other people, both in your personal life and at work? How have these reactions helped or hindered their trust in you? Similarly, what emotions do others provoke in you, and how has your trust level been affected?
- How often do you "go it alone" to get things done and make things happen? How does that approach affect you in achieving your goals in your personal and professional life?

CHAPTER 10

Read This Last

I teach and coach people from all walks of life all over the world. Everywhere I go, I encounter people who are highly successful in the world, living the "good" life but lacking true spiritual abundance. While they appear to be living "the lifestyle of the rich and famous" on the outside, I find that people are hurting and broken on the inside.

Living life in abundance is about living a vibrant, exciting life in Christ, and it goes hand in hand with developing a personal relationship with Him. Jesus wants us to be in love with Him. The concepts and principles of this book are intended to teach you and guide you into that kind of personal relationship with Jesus.

So, let me take you back to where we began in this book. To have an abundant life in Jesus you must have a personal relationship with Him. That relationship begins with a heart of contrition and repentance. It begins with the acknowledgement that you cannot live life as the master of your own destiny. You must be able to admit that there really is no such thing as "self-help." Accepting personal responsibility and accountability means that you confess your faults and sins and admit that Jesus must become Lord of your life so His blood can cleanse you of all unrighteousness. Without Jesus as our advocate, we live a life earning the wages of sin, which is death (Rom. 6:23).

The journey to an abundant life in Jesus begins with spiritual healing. We were born into sin, and we need to be reborn in the Spirit.

This journey begins by cultivating a personal relationship with Jesus Christ and the Father through the power of the Holy Spirit. Salvation is an act that occurs in a moment in time and leads to our spiritual transformation, which is a continual process of change into the nature, character, and image of Jesus Christ. This journey requires that you live life with intentional purpose, setting your will to live a life of holiness and to reject sin and the temptations of this world.

Along the way, using the concepts of this book, you can learn and apply the daily practice of taking every thought captive. You can learn and apply the principles of this book to purposefully manage your thoughts, emotions, attitude, and actions. The Holy Spirit will reveal the faulty thinking and mental patterns you have acquired during your lifetime. When you decide that you are ready to change, the Holy Spirit can replace all the ungodly elements of your mind, will, and emotions with godly and holy elements of thought, emotions, attitude, and actions. By engaging in praise and prayer, you can then release the power of God to bring transformational change into your life. In this process you will experience a mental and emotional healing from all the dysfunctional baggage you have accumulated in your life experiences. You will exchange a life lived in spiritual scarcity for a life lived in spiritual abundance. The choice is yours, so choose wisely.

The journey can begin now with this prayer: "Father, I am thankful for all the painful events of my life. I praise You in Your wisdom that You have brought me to this moment in time to transform my life. I accept responsibility for the ineffective choices and destructive habits of my life. I am truly sorry for waiting so long to submit to You as the Lord of my life. I am thankful for Your mercy in waiting for me to confess and commit to a holy life in Jesus Christ. Thank You for Your love and for Your mercy and forgiveness to me. I accept Jesus Christ as Lord and Savior of my life. I give my life to You and pray that You will teach me and lead me into right thinking, emotions, and behavior, that I may live my life in spiritual abundance by the power of the Holy Spirit. Thank you for saving me, redeeming me, and transforming me into the nature and image of Your Son, my Lord and Savior, Jesus Christ. In the name of Jesus, I pray, amen.

APPENDIX 1

Social / Behavioral Styles under Stress

Recognize and Adapt

Even very effective communicators will find it challenging to adapt their behaviors under stress. Emotional management makes a difference in your performance, relationships, and overall happiness. All of us experience moments when unwanted emotions intensify, and that's normal. It's what you do with them that can lead to problems at work, at home, and in your spiritual life.

However, those who learn to be aware of the weaknesses and blind spots in themselves and others know how to recognize the signs of behavioral styles under stress and to adapt themselves more quickly, turning their weaknesses back into the strengths of their behavioral style. Can you identify which pattern most dominates your behavior under stress? To learn more about behavioral and social styles, you can do an Internet search by typing in key words—like *social styles*, *behavior patterns*, or *DISC profile*—as a starting point to discover more about your own behavior pattern. You can also e-mail me for more information as well.

Style 1: The *Driver* Responds to Challenges and Problems

Under stress, the *driver* is demanding, nervy, aggressive, and egotistical.

- Micromanaging
- Confrontational
- Demanding
- Angry
- Inflexible
- Imposing upon others, demanding to lead, unyielding and uncompromising

Consider this: how would a *driver* under stress respond to problems and challenges?

Style 2: The *Expressive* Person Persuades Others to His or Her Point of View

Under stress, the *expressive* person is self-promoting, overly optimistic, gabby, glib, and unrealistic.

- Oversells
- Shifts blame
- Confronts
- Attacks
- Is loud, boisterous, and sarcastic
- Expresses and verbalizes judgmental feelings

Consider this: How would an *expressive* person under stress interact with others?

Style 3: The *Amiable* Person Responds to the Pace of the Environment

Under stress, the *amiable* person is undemonstrative, unconcerned, hesitant, and inflexible.

- Gives in
- Exhibits flat emotions in facial expressions and gestures
- Lacks commitment though voicing agreement
- Becomes passive-aggressive
- Complies rather than cooperates, producing minimal results
- Is slow to forgive in conflict and will backstab

Consider this: how would an *amiable* person under stress respond to changes in environmental pace?

Style 4: The *Analytical* Person Responds to Rules and Procedures

Under stress, the *analytical* person is pessimistic, picky/fussy, and overly critical.

- Becomes nonresponsive
- Takes an avoidance approach to people and conflict
- Delays actions and decisions, becoming hypercritical and hypersensitive
- Retreats to working on other issues or projects
- Withdraws emotionally and interpersonally, adopting a victim mentality
- Limits all vocal, facial, and other body-language gestures

Consider this: how would an *analytical* person under stress respond to changes in procedures and rules?

APPENDIX 2

Assess the Trust Levels in Your Team Relationships

Team relationships can be personal family relationships, work relationships, and church relationships.

Rate each statement below using this key: "0" if the statement does not apply, "1" if you do not agree, "2" if you agree slightly, and "3" if you agree completely. Then tally the ratings and find the corresponding score at the end of this tool.

1. All members of the team are accountable and take responsibility for their actions, words, and responsibilities. _____
2. Team communication is open, with information-sharing, team problem-solving and analysis, and honest discourse without fear of retaliation. _____
3. The team leader is not a micromanager and regularly shows confidence in and respect for the team. _____
4. All team members are engaged in their tasks and are interested in participating. _____
5. No side deals or flouting of team-established rules, if known, are tolerated. _____

6. Every team member, including the leader, does what he or she says. _____
7. The team leader provides the necessary resources (e.g., insight, information, time, staff, money, training) to enable the team to achieve its goals. _____
8. All team members are regarded as contributors (not just bodies) whose skills, knowledge, and abilities add value to the team. _____
9. The team culture emphasizes interdependency, encouraging cooperation and collaboration among members. _____
10. Attitudinal and behavioral conflicts are dealt with immediately. _____

Ratings total: _____

Score key:

1–10 = no or low level of trust: minimal cooperation and minimal collaboration

11–20 = acceptable level of trust: some cooperation and some collaboration

21–30 = high level of trust: high cooperation and high collaboration

References

Cloud, Henry. *Boundaries for Leaders*. New York: Harper Collins, 2013.

Senge, Peter M. *The Fifth Discipline*. New York: Doubleday, 1990.

Johnston, Ray. *The Hope Quotient*. Nashville: W Publishing, 2014.

Leaf, Caroline. *Who Switched Off My Brain?* Nashville: Thomas Nelson, 2009.

Quinn, Robert. *Deep Change*. San Francisco: John Wiley & Sons, 1996.

Maltz, Maxwell. *Psycho-Cybernetics*. New York: Penguin Group, 2001.

Seamands, David A. *Healing for Damaged Emotions*. Colorado Springs: Cook, 2004.

Stanley, Charles F. *Emotions*. New York: Howard Books, 2013.

Smalley, Gary. *Change Your Heart, Change Your Life*. Nashville: Thomas Nelson, 2007.

Kight, Tim. *The R-Factor*. Columbus, Ohio: Focus3, 2007.

Frisina, Michael E. *Influential Leadership*. Chicago: HealthCare Administration Press, 2014.

Patterson, Kerry, Joseph Grenny, David Maxfield, Ron McMillan, and Al Switzler. *Influencer: The Power to Change Anything.* VitalSmarts, LLC, 2008.

Schwartz, Barry, and Kenneth Sharpe. *Practical Wisdom.* Riverhead Books, 2010.

About the Author

Michel E. Frisina served as a career military officer in the United States Army Medical Department. He served in a variety of positions of increasing responsibility to include teaching positions at the United States Military Academy at West Point and the Uniformed Services University of Health Sciences and Medical School at Bethesda, Maryland.

Transitioning to civilian health care administration, Michael held a number of leadership positions in several health care systems, most noteworthy as the Director for Cardiovascular Services, Providence Hospitals and Vascular Institute. During this time, Michael founded Calvary Chapel Northeast Columbia to begin his pastoral ministry.

Michael is an expository teacher of the Holy Bible with the purpose of leading people to Jesus, growing them up in Jesus, and sending them out to serve for the gospel of Jesus Christ. Michael continues to serve in his health care calling, and he serves primarily as a leadership development speaker and executive coach for the American College of Health Care Executives.

He is married to the former Susan Gail Weston. They have three adult children—Michael, Robert, and Rebekah—and five grandchildren. The family resides in South Carolina.

CPSIA information can be obtained at www.ICGtesting.com
Printed in the USA
BVOW04s2316220916

463049BV00002B/3/P